George T. Wolz

February 26, 1974

MOUNDS, TOWNS AND TOTEMS

MOUNDS,

Illustrated by W. T. Mars

TOWNS AND TOTEMS

Indians of North America

ROBERT MYRON

THE WORLD PUBLISHING COMPANY

CLEVELAND AND NEW YORK

To my wonderful wife, Marie-Rose

Published by The World Publishing Company
2231 West 110th Street, Cleveland, Ohio 44102
Published simultaneously in Canada by
Nelson, Foster & Scott Ltd.
Library of Congress catalog card number: 66-10639
HL66

CONTENTS

FOREWORD

Our common history began not at Plymouth but in the heartland of America. Some of the artificial hills of earth left in this country by the mound-building Indians date back to the time of Christ. The prototypes of today's urban dwellings are not the medieval towns of Europe, but our own Pueblo apartments of the Southwest. And in their totems, the Indian expressed almost the whole range of ideas known to man.

The Mound Builders were preoccupied with life hereafter; the Indians of the Plains, with annual rejuvenations around the buffalo hunt; the Iroquois, with political forms responsive to European invaders. These themes of death, life, and power can be found in every major civilization, but even more prominent among the Indians was their tireless search for the good life. The Indian struggled to maintain his heritage of freedom against the threat of those determined to take his land and unwilling to accept his culture.

Much more than a history of Indian life, this book also illuminates our contemporary search to understand ourselves. If American values had been different, instead of isolating the Indian we might have used him as a bridge to help us reach and understand indigenous peoples elsewhere. Our earliest and most sustained wrongs have been against the Indian, and we can allow their descendants to develop only by accepting as our own the values and goals of freedom and respect they hold most dear.

LAWRENCE C. HOWARD
University of Wisconsin

MOUNDS, TOWNS AND TOTEMS

SETTING THE STAGE

The Indian has been the subject of more fiction, folklore, and films than any other American. Despite his popularity, he remains the least understood and most misrepresented of all. Although labeled "Indian," he is not from India; although called "Red Man," he is not red; although romanticized as "The Noble Savage," his behavior has sometimes been neither noble nor savage. American Indians are an extraordinary diversity of peoples as individualistic as the ancestors of Americans who came from Europe, Asia, or Africa.

Physically, most American Indians seem to have belonged to the Mongoloid race related to peoples of Asia, rather than to the Caucasian Europeans. Physiques and complexions varied from place to place and from tribe to tribe. Indians shared no common language, except possibly that of signs. Like Europeans, they spoke different tongues, wore different clothes, created different art forms, worshiped different gods. Some tribes lived in makeshift tepees; others gardened and herded; some specialized in bead and feather work; others built large apartment houses; some hunted and fished; others carved effigy pipes and fearsome masks; some made painted pottery; some had primitive rule; others perfected an organized government so democratic in spirit that it inspired Benjamin Franklin when he planned the Federation of States.

The fascinating story of our Indian heritage unfolded centuries before the landing of Columbus and the greatest mistake in nomenclature in all history, the "Indians."

The story begins about thirty thousand years ago when Alaska was still joined to the Asian mainland at what is now the Bering Strait. Ancestors of the Indian people wandered out of Asia and crossed the cold wastelands without knowing whether they were in Asia or North America. These first comers gradually worked their way down the west coast and along the foothills of the Rocky Mountains. In time, some of them crossed the Rio Grande into Mexico, found their way down the twisted Isthmus of Panama into South America until they eventually reached Tierra del Fuego, the cold dreary tip of the Hemisphere.

The circuitous journey from the Bering Strait to Tierra del Fuego must have taken these hardy pioneers thousands of years to achieve. With the passing of time, they increased in number and perfected their weapons, tools, and techniques of obtaining food. Some learned to select the wild but edible grasses and plants of the fields and forests. From foraging for food, some progressed to the planting and harvesting of corn, beans, squash, and other crops. Whether as hunters or fishermen, foragers or farmers, these Indians soon gained a foothold in America and formed distinct tribes. Their customs and culture were affected by the climate and environment that they confronted in different regions of the country.

Hugging the fertile valleys and tributaries of the sprawling Ohio and Mississippi Rivers, were the mound-building Indians. Hunters, fishermen, and gardeners, these industrious people built thousands of earthen mounds over the burial places of their dead. They also heaped up earth into many different geometric, animal, and even human shapes of colossal size. These mound-building Indians were the greatest artists of ancient North America. They carved and modeled an amazing variety of forms and styles. Other mound-building Indians in the Southeast near the Gulf Coast, influenced by the Pre-Columbian builders of Mexico, built pyramidal mounds topped with wooden shrines, where their priests did homage to their gods.

The Natchez Indians of Mississippi may have been descended directly from these mound builders. As far as we know, they were the only American Indians to have a king, an aristocracy, and common people bound together by complex rituals and rules. Early investigators from Europe recorded that the Natchez king ruled by the will of the people, a tradition that some believe may have influenced our political concept of a government by consent of the governed.

Far to the north, Iroquois tribes built compact palisaded villages in New York State, the Great Lakes and the St. Lawrence River region. Over this land of hard, snowy winters, the Iroquois hunted and farmed, shared a common language, recorded some of their legends and history and their deep religious convictions. They formed a strong political confederacy called the League of Six Nations. About one thousand Iroquois still survive in New York State and strive to maintain the traditions of the ancestral League.

West of the Mississippi, the vast flat area bordered by the Rocky Mountains to the west and extending from Canada southward almost to the Rio Grande is known as the Great Plains. This was the great grazing area of North America. Here the Sioux, Blackfoot, Crow, Cheyenne, Comanche, and other tribes pitched their skin tepees and hunted buffalo. These dashing Indians recorded their exploits on the cured hides of the buffaloes. They also perfected the handicrafts of bead, quill, and feather work. Tribal life was shattered and scattered by the invasion of the westward moving wagon trains of the pioneering white men. Popular knowledge of the Indian has been based on tales of battles fought between Plains Indians and white frontiersmen.

Southward, on the torrid sun-baked plains of Arizona, New Mexico, and parts of Utah and Colorado, are the extensive towns of the Pueblo Indians. Like most urban dwellers, these Indians inhabited apartment houses. Some were built of adobe out in the open; others were constructed or excavated in the crevices of cliffs. To maintain these towns in the semidesert, the Pueblos carried on a daily round of digging canals for irrigation, cultivating and rotating crops and performing religious rituals such as ceremonial dances for successful production. Because the dry climate has preserved many ancient remains, more is known about the early history of the Indians of the Southwest than about the history of Indians in other parts of the country. The descendants who live there today still practice the ancestral ways and speak the same language as did their forefathers. These Indians also made fine pottery, raised and wove cotton and wool, and fashioned excellent jewelry of turquoise and shell.

In contrast with Pueblo Indians, were the Northwest Coast tribes who inhabited the coastal area of what is now northern California, Washington, Oregon, British Columbia, and Alaska. In this moderate-to-chilly region of dense rainfall, the Indians had little agriculture, but they established a culture based on fishing and forestry. With easy access to the sea and rivers, there was excellent fishing for salmon, seals, and whales. In the dense forests they hunted a great variety of game. From the trees they built villages of decorated wooden houses, hewed out giant canoes, and converted the bark into woven textiles. They reveled in religious rituals and colorful ceremonies as complex as the names of the tribes themselves—Kwakiutl, Tlingit, Haida, Nootka. Towering above the villages were the spectacular totem poles, carved and brightly painted stylized images of birds, animals, and fish.

Mound builders, cliff dwellers, totem-pole artists; hunters, farmers, fishermen—there was great diversity among the tribes and between them and their contemporaries in other regions of the continent. Their monuments stand as silent testimony of the richly vital life and culture of the American Indians long before the Europeans came and conquered the land.

MOUNDS FOR THE DEAD

From the Atlantic Coast to the Rocky Mountains of North America, more than one hundred thousand Indian earthen monuments, made in an amazing variety of forms, have been found. Some are conical, some pyramidal; others are serpentine and shaped like birds or beasts. Some are hilltop ramparts, others have geometric walls enclosing many acres. Today, some mounds are hardly distinguishable hillocks overgrown with grass or trees, blending into the landscape. Others are better preserved and truly imposing. These structures were made without brick or stone, without horsepower, without wheels. The Mound Builders laboriously piled up these massive structures with earth that they dug, lugged, and dumped by might and muscle, workable season after season, year after year. The primitive organization and planning involved may be compared with the efforts that must have gone into the construction of Egyptian or Mexican pyramids. Like pyramids, these earthworks reveal the power of the ruler and his priests as well as the ceremonial traditions of a populous tribe.

Just as these structures take many forms, so were they built not by one, but by a series of separate Indian cultures spanning more than twenty-five hundred years. Archaeologists divide the history of the Mound Builders into two periods: the Burial Mound Indians of the Ohio Valley, *c.* 1000 B.C. to *c.* A.D. 800, and the Temple Mound Indians further to the south along the banks of the Mississippi River and its major tributaries, *c.* A.D. 700 to *c.* A.D. 1600.

The earlier Burial Mound culture is called Adena, after the estate of William Worthington, former governor of Ohio, where a typical mound was discovered. Distributed through southern Ohio, northern Kentucky, and the western part of West Virginia, the Adena conical-shaped mounds were for burials. Sometimes these mounds were enclosed with circular walls for funeral ceremonials. Most of them range from ten to twenty feet in height, but the famous Grave Creek Mound in Moundsville, West Virgina, is over seventy feet high and is one of the tallest mounds known to have been built by Indian tribes of North America.

What little is known about the Adena and other Mound Building Indians has been learned largely from the character and content of the mounds. When the spade of the archaeologist sliced into the mound, it usually revealed pockets of white ash. Identified as human remains, these finds confirmed the belief that most of the Adena dead were cremated. Only a few people, such as important priests, chiefs, and members of his family, were bodily entombed. Graves for these honored dead were made in tombs dug in the floor of the house. The body was wrapped in a simple woven shroud, placed on a bed of bark strips, and sprinkled with red ochre, a color that symbolized the revitalizing spirit of the afterlife. Skeletons of others found nearby were probably those of relatives or dependents, killed and buried in the belief common among primitive people that they or their spirit would accompany their chief to the other world. For use in the future existence, weapons, tools, ornaments, and even statues were "killed" or broken before being placed in the tomb. Then a small heap of earth was placed over the remains, the house set afire, and the final large mound built over the ashes.

The Adena house has been reconstructed from the foundation

found beneath the burial mound. It was circular in plan, between twenty and seventy feet in diameter. The walls were constructed of a framework of poles. These were set in pairs for greater strength, about four feet apart and inclined outward at the top so as to shed rain water away from the walls. Spaces between the posts may have been filled in with tightly woven twigs and branches, the whole presumably plastered over with a mixture of clay and chopped twigs or reeds for better protection from the weather. Several window openings may have been left for ventilation, as well as a single entranceway which usually faced southeast. Four to six posts were also set near the center of the house as roof supports. The roofs may have been made of overlapping strips of bark resting on a network of vines and sinew lines. A small opening was left at the top to permit the smoke from the stone fireplace to escape.

No home furnishings have survived. More than likely, the Adena slept on beds of grass and used animal skins and furs for blankets. That they sat on their heels, like other Indian tribes, is revealed by the distinctive deformations of leg bones found in many skeletons.

The actual height of the house cannot be determined, but the deeply imbedded poles suggest that it might have been as much as fifteen feet high. It was in this type of house, perhaps with minor modifications, that most Mound Building Indians lived. While far from spacious or comfortable by our standards, it satisfied the needs of a people who spent most of their lives out-of-doors.

The Adena were the first Indians to farm the Ohio Valley. They cultivated beans, squash, and perhaps corn, although traces of kernels or cobs are scanty. Beans and squash grow wild in many regions of North America, but corn did not originate in this region. Research has revealed that the first cultivation of corn was far to the south in Middle or South America. Knowledge of corn and its cultivation could have spread northward from village to village until it reached the Ohio Valley. It is not known if corn became a part of the Adena culture, but village refuse proves that these people gathered and ate such strange but nourishing plants as catary grass, pawpaw, goosefoot, honey locust, marsh elder, giant ragweed. Sunflower seeds were a special favorite and were consumed in large quantities. Hunting and fishing, however, provided the major supply of food, evidenced by the discarded shells and countless animal bones accumulated about the cooking fires.

This well-organized Adena culture did not spring overnight from the minds of a few progressive Indians. Many of their ways of doing and making things came from a more ancient culture, called by scholars the Archaic Culture. Its participants are believed to date as far back as the end of the Ice Age, around 8000 B.C. The Adena Indians inhabited the same territory as the Archaic people, and for a time the two lived side by side trading and sharing materials and methods. But the Archaic Indians were not cultivators of the soil or builders of mounds, they were food gatherers. They foraged for the wild fruits of the forest—for seeds, roots, berries, and nuts.

And along the banks of the Ohio and Mississippi Rivers, they gathered and devoured vast beds of freshwater shellfish. Generation after generation, the discarded shells collected to form huge piles as deep as twenty feet and spread over an area of more than fifty acres. The Archaic Indians often built their villages upon these shell heaps, and here they lived, died, and were buried.

Campsites on these riverside shell heaps had crude dwellings. Some were merely makeshift lean-tos; others were cone-shaped teepees or a more primitive version of the circular Adena house. With bone harpoons, crude nets of fibers, and elaborate weirs, the campers captured fish from the fast-flowing streams. Wild animals coming to the rivers to drink fell before the sharp pointed spears of the Archaic Indians. These were powerfully thrown by the ingenious invention of the spear-hurler, which was actually an arm extender consisting of a wooden shaft about two feet long, an antler hook about six inches long, and a hollowed stone weight. The hunter fitted the end of his spear against the antler hook, steadied it in place with the fingers of his throwing hand, and threw the spear by jerking his hand forcibly forward. The spear sped ahead to its target with increased momentum while the spear-hurler stayed in the hunter's hand. By this device the Archaic Indian could throw his spear further, faster, and straighter than he could by hand.

To give the spear-hurler proper balance, weights were delicately carved from pieces of chert, limestone, or flint and highly polished. These so-called bannerstones were truly works of art with lovely coloration and porcelainesque surfaces. The Archaic Indian artists carved other stones known as birdstones into the streamlined shapes of birds, curiously modern in style but unknown in meaning. The Adena hunter adopted the spear-hurler, "atlatl" (an Aztec word), but his bannerstone weights never attained the artistic quality of those of the Archaic craftsmen.

From the Archaic Indians, the Adena craftsmen also learned the use of copper, how to make pottery, and perhaps the habit of smoking tobacco. Copper was mined in the region of Lake

Superior before 5000 B.C. and found its way into the Archaic Indian villages of the Mississippi Valley centuries before its use was common in Europe. Whereas copper encouraged the cultural progress in Europe and Asia, it scarcely changed the pattern of American Indian life, because they used it as a stone rather than as a metal. American Indians never tried smelting or casting copper, and they did not combine it with other ingredients to make bronze. Instead they hammered it into many different shapes, a procedure that did not reveal copper's many other potential uses. They never advanced to a Bronze Age in the generally accepted use of that term.

From Archaic sites in the Southeast, the Adena Indians probably learned, through trade and contacts, the methods and techniques of pottery making. They found that certain clays mixed with water into a thick paste could be rolled or pinched into a long thin strand, then formed into a tight spiral for the base of a vessel. The sides were built up with additional strands until the desired width and shape of a container had been made. Since the potter's wheel was unknown to the North American Indian, all his pots and pans were fashioned by this hand-coiling method. The surfaces of the pottery were smoothed with hand and wooden paddle and then baked at a low temperature in a slow-burning wood or dung fire. Archaic pottery, however, was crude, coarse, and heavy because of the sand and vegetable fibers used in mixing the clay. The Adena potters improved upon the technique and materials. They added pulverized shells or potsherds to the clay and learned to control the firing temperatures. Adena pottery had thinner walls and smoother surfaces, which were sometimes decorated with geometric designs. Some of the choicer Adena vessels were made exclusively for ceremonial purpose and for placement with the dead in the grave mounds.

The Archaic Indians may have been the world's first smokers. Hollow stone tubes from their shell mounds apparently were smoking pipes. Similarly shaped stone pipes have been unearthed in Adena graves. While smoking may have offered the Indian relaxation and enjoyment, it probably played a more significant role in his religious observances. Like incense, the bitter aromatic tobacco smoke, ascending upward, was an offering to the gods. The ceremonial long-stemmed pipe, or calumet, became the well-known symbol of diplomacy and friendship among many Indian tribes.

A ceremonial pipe, an extraordinary carving, was recovered from the Ohio mound from which the Adena culture derived its name. Basically tubular in shape, it was carved in the image of a free-standing male Indian, eight inches tall and weighing more than one pound. The smoke channel was drilled through the figure with an opening at the top of the head. The chunky muscular body was carved with a breech-cloth decorated with a feathered bustle at the rear and serpentine design engraved on the front. The hair was similar in style to that of later Indian braves, close cut on the sides of the head with a cockscomb at the top parted and combed to either side. The lobes of the ears were distended by large hollow plugs, obviously a means of enhancement. The deep-set eyes and open mouth gave a dramatic expression. Not only is this the only human figure known in Adena art, it is quite different in style from the art of all other Mound Building Indians thus far discovered. The Adena pipe is shrouded in mystery and has puzzled archaeologists for many years.

About a dozen engraved stone tablets, more typical of Adena art, have been recovered from different mounds. These limestone slabs were cut into rectangular and oval shapes and decorated on one side with a complicated design of two confronting hawks or other birds of prey. Only the heads and hooked beaks were clearly delineated; wings, talons, and feathers were portrayed in intricate abstract patterns. Often the body of the bird was represented as a sinuous serpent. That these tablets may have been used as stamps, covered with paint and pressed against the body or clothing, is suggested by traces of red pigment adhering to some of the tablets. Some of these Adena designs inspired other tribal craftsmen, especially the Hopewell who inhabited the region at a later time.

Unlike the Adena, the Archaic Indians did not build burial mounds, but they did share an intense concern about death and the afterlife. They put the corpse in the grave together with tools and implements and also practiced cremation. Graves were usually small pits so narrow that the body had to be crammed in. Sometimes the corpse was folded accordian fashion and secured with a cord, possibly to prevent his spirit from returning to haunt his enemies or the homes of his former villagers.

A comparison of skeletons reveals physical distinctions between the Archaic and Adena Indians. The skulls of the Archaic Indians generally were of the longheaded type, whereas Adena skulls belonged to a more roundheaded group. Many Adena skulls, unlike the Archaic, were purposefully deformed in shape, a trait common to many Mound Building Indians. The head of an infant was strapped against a wooden cradleboard so that as the child grew the back of its head was flattened and the forehead given a depressed shape. The reason for deformation of the skulls is uncertain. It might have been a sign of social status or simply a tribal taste or fashion.

It is generally conceded that Adena Indians were stockier, stronger, and less subject to the infirmities of their Archaic forebears. Examination of hundreds of skeletons reveals that one out of every two Archaic Indians suffered from arthritis. The disease is easily recognized by the hard, smoothly worn ends of elbow and knee joints caused by constant rubbing whenever the limbs moved. This friction was the source of agonizing pain to the arthritic victim. Their diet and the lack of calcium contributed to the Archaic Indians' serious dental problems. Some teeth were worn down to the level of the gums; others were eroded with deep abscesses; many more had fallen out from decay. The more balanced diet of the Adena people prevented many of these physical problems.

Spadework and study have unlocked many secret doors to the Adena past, but the story is incomplete and many questions remain unanswered. The origin of the Adena Indian has been a perennial subject of controversy among scholars. Some believe that the Adena Indians originated in Mexico or Central America and migrated northward to the Ohio Valley with a full-blown culture. Agriculture, mound building, and skull deformation are factors contributing to this theory. No culture remotely resembling the Adena has been found, however, anywhere south of Kentucky. On the other hand, many of the roots of Adena culture are to be found among Archaic Indians. Any Mexican or southern traits, more than likely, were the result of sporadic trade or contacts with a few individuals whose journeys may have been prompted by numerous factors. Perhaps future archaeological work in the mound region will throw light on these questions.

Whatever the origin of the Adena Indians, it is certain that they were the first to build burial mounds in North America and that they set the stage for the achievements of later Indian tribes.

EARTHWORKS AND EFFIGIES

Sometime around 100 B.C. a band of longheaded Indians wandered into the region of what is now the state of Ohio. Their uneventful arrival was witnessed by the Adena Indians. The newcomers were from southern Illinois, where villages and modest burial mounds testify to their early presence and possible descent from the Archaic Indians. The reason for this eastward migration is unknown, but once they settled in southern Ohio, these Indians spawned one of the most impressive cultures of ancient North America. Archaeologists call it the Hopewell culture because excavation of a number of their burial mounds was made on land once owned by H. C. Hopewell. Great Earthwork Builders would be a more appropriate name.

The most striking assemblage of Hopewell mounds and earthworks was near the banks of the great Ohio River and its major tributaries—the Miami, Scioto, and the Muskingum Rivers. In this now quiet farming community, more than five hundred burial mounds and miles of walled embankments stand as proof of the existence of a mighty and industrious population some two thousand years ago.

Many of the Hopewell mounds are dome-shaped, clustered to-

gether, and enclosed by earthen walls in square, circular, octagonal, and parallel-line patterns. The dimensions of some enclosures are immense: earthen walls near the town of Newark, Ohio, cover four square miles. Many of the burial mounds range between 20 and 30 feet in height and extend from 160 to 470 feet in length.

Mounds and surrounding walls were not the only structures built by the Hopewell Indians in this part of Ohio. Elaborate ceremonies must have been performed at the famous Serpent Mound near the town of Peebles. Atop a high ridge overlooking a river, the Indians molded from the earth the replica of a gigantic serpent, 20 feet wide, 5 feet high, and extending 1331 feet, over a quarter of a mile, or more than the height of the Empire State Building. Within the stylized shape of the head a fire burned in a ceremonial altar while Indians gathered on the surrounding embankment. Seen from the air, the serpent seems to glide in and out of the forested terrain like some nightmarish apparition.

About A.D. 550, the Hopewell Indians erected ramparts on several prominent hilltops in southern Ohio. These were probably places of refuge from marauding tribes. Fort Hill and Fort Miami are typical examples; Fort Ancient, near Wilmington, is the largest known. Here tremendous earthwork walls rise like a mighty fortress 270 feet above the edge of a plateau that dominates the area. The walls curve and bend almost four miles and after centuries of erosion still range from six to twenty feet high. It has been estimated that more than 628,800 cubic yards of earth were moved by Indians in building it. Most of the earth was heaped up leaving a ditch paralleling the wall, which was reinforced at less solid places with stone slabs.

Southern Ohio was the cultural capital of the Hopewell. From here their influence radiated outward. Similar but smaller mound sites were built as far as the Rockies, eastward to the Atlantic seaboard, and southward into Florida. These sites were probably outposts.

Trading became a highly organized activity among the Ohio Hopewell Indians. Exotic materials were transported along the well-established trade routes—obsidian from what is now Yellowstone Park for ceremonial spear points; claws and large eyeteeth from Rocky Mountain bears for necklaces and buttons; mica from Virgina, the Carolinas, and Alabama; copper ore from the Lake Superior region, and conch shells, the teeth of sharks, and the bones of alligator and barracuda from Florida and the Gulf Coast. From the rivers and streams in Ohio, the Hopewell collected freshwater pearls. All these materials were used in many decorative and functional forms.

Priests and chieftains demanded furnishings for their graves. The Hopewell, like the Adena Indians, cremated most of their dead; but unlike the Adena, they entombed many more bodies within their mounds, indicative perhaps of a greater population. They must have had morgues for storing the corpses, because it is unlikely that so many people would have died at any one time. The bodies may have been stored high in the trees as later Indian tribes are known to have done, or else stored away until the occasion for mass burial. Some bodies were given a simple burial. Others, evidently important chieftains or priests, were buried with considerable pomp and ceremony. For these, graves were built of logs and occasionally reinforced with stone slabs. The body, dressed in colorfully dyed garments decorated with freshwater pearls and bear-teeth buttons, was placed on a shiny bed of mica. Heavy necklaces of shells or pearls were hung around the neck while copper bracelets encircled the wrists and arms. Copper spools were inserted into the earlobes, and breastplates of copper rested on the chest. Particularly esteemed rulers were crowned with a copper headdress surmounted with antler horns, an impressive symbol of high office.

Many possessions of the dead were placed in the grave—tools, weapons, pottery, sculpture, and huge conch shells. Decapitated skulls found near the arms of the corpse may have been trophy heads of vanquished enemies or relics of relatives or friends. As an extra tribute, some bodies were completely surrounded from head to feet with thousands of freshwater pearls. Near the graves archaeologists have found small pits containing excellent carvings. In compliance with custom, many of these carved objects had been ceremonially "killed" before being deposited in the pits, which were full to overflowing. The Turner Mound, near Cincinnati, contained 22,000 shell beads, 48,000 pearls, 700 copper beads, 2,000 canine teeth, 600 pieces of selected animal bone, and 12 alligator teeth.

The construction of the Hopewell burial mounds must have required much time, care, and labor. Many months must have passed while the graves were being fitted and furnished. An extensive wooden structure was required to house a large colony of the dead. This would be five feet or more in height, some fifty feet in width, and up to two hundred feet in length, requiring around six hundred wooden posts. The plan was divided into a number of compartments, some of which may have been roofed.

One can imagine, when all was readied for the dedication, some Indians selected for the ritual stepping forward with flaming torches and igniting the great funeral structure. As the hungry flames soared upward, mobs of Indians danced around the blazing pyre, their rapid movements frantically trying to keep in rhythm with the increasing tempo of the chanting, singing, shouting mass of participants in the primitive ceremony. Then suddenly there came a halt as a magnificently robed priest stepped forth on a raised platform, raised his arms, and commanded the people to consecrate a memorial to their departed ruler and kinfolk. In the hushed silence, long rows of Indians moved back and forth between the outskirts of the village where the earth had been freshly dug, and the charred graves where they dumped their baskets of earth on the slowly rising mound. Like the pantheons and cathedrals of later days, these Hopewell mounds received the mortal remains of great men.

Little has survived of the many Hopewell villages. One reason for this disappointing lack is that earthworks were built on high ground, while villages grew in the more convenient and fertile bottom lands along the river banks. When the rivers periodically overflowed, the villages might be washed away and all traces of them lost under accumulations of silt that formed the river flood plains. From the evidence that has survived, it is believed that the Hopewell Indians inhabited houses much like those of the Adena tribes, and that the villages themselves were small farming communities. In the rich river soil they raised corn, beans, squash. But like their Adena forebears, they depended for their food primarily on hunting. The white-tailed deer was the favorite meat, with the cottontail rabbit and wild turkey close rivals, judging from the bone deposits around cooking-sites and campsites. Fish, turtles, and many species of mollusks or shellfish, together with nuts, berries, and wild plums, were gathered from the life-sustaining streams and forests.

The Hopewell villages enjoyed an ample food supply and growing population. There was not only adequate manpower for the

monumental earthworks being built, but much leisure time for the development and perfection of arts and crafts. Hopewell craftsmen in southern Ohio produced artistic carvings that rate among the best art made by ancient man anywhere in the world.

Of the many living creatures portrayed in their carvings, it was the duck hawk that most dramatically captured the artists' imagination. This bird of prey was the peregrine falcon, the most ferocious member of the hawk family, an American cousin of the hunting falcon immortalized in song and poetry during the Middle Ages in Europe. One of the swiftest and fiercest birds of prey, the duck hawk can dive at a speed estimated to exceed 170 miles an hour. The bird symbolized the speed and prowess demanded of Hopewell hunters, although the idea and image of the hawk may have been inspired by Adena tablets. Its image appeared in practically every material used by the Hopewell artists—copper, mica, bone, stone, shell, and the surface of clay pottery. Sometimes the duck hawk was represented with remarkable realism; at other times it was abstracted into complex designs. Regardless of how shown, its distinctive features were large eye, toothed beak, heavy wing, and sometimes enormous pointed talons.

In addition to recognizable animal forms, there was a rich variety of abstract motifs, many of which were derived from plant forms. A sense of symmetry, refined rhythmic lines, the selection of the essentials of the subject depicted, and an extraordinary creative imagination distinguish Hopewell engravings.

The Hopewell improved upon the Adena smoking pipe and perfected a distinctive platform pipe that had a thin curved pedestal with gracefully rounded bowl rising in the center. The stone platform pipe has been found at so many Hopewell sites that it is the hallmark of the culture. When the bowl of these pipes was carved in the shape of some living form, it became an "effigy pipe." No larger than the palm of one's hand, the miniature figures are amazingly lifelike. Hawks and crows threaten to fly away; otters and mountain lions seem ready to dash off the platform; raccoons or blue herons, clutching and eating fish, were caught in the act of seeking food. With keen observation of nature and mastery of his materials, the Hopewell artist imparted to the inanimate stones a sense of life and movement. He often heightened the feeling of life with an exquisite linear treatment of skin, fur, and feathers, using pearls or copper to enliven the sparkle of the eyes. The effigy pipes provide a zoological collection of the bird and small animal life that inhabited the Ohio Valley more than two thousand years ago.

The Hopewell Indian also carved images of himself on smoking pipes. Serious, unsmiling faces, they look out with large, open, yet sightless eyes. Some faces are richly tattooed; others bear elaborate headdresses that perhaps indicated priests, chieftains, or warriors. Two groups of full-length standing clay figures, from the Hopewell mounds of Illinois and Ohio, depict women wearing knee-length wraparound skirts; men with a brief loincloth. Both wore moccasins, but some men also had leggings, perhaps for long hunting or trading expeditions. Women combed their hair straight back and tied it in a chignon; the men often tied their hair into one or more knots above the forehead. Decorative armbands, necklaces, ear-spools, and colorful body painting were all vital parts of their dress.

The sculptor penetrated beyond the surface, and defined the Indians' distinctive Mongoloid characteristics, high cheekbones and narrow slanted eyes, as well as their artificially deformed skulls. Women were shown heavier and stockier than the men, which is not surprising in view of all the work they were expected to perform in the village or on long treks. Most moving are the effigies of two women tenderly holding and comforting their children. Maternal feelings were rarely portrayed by Indian artists, or by primitive peoples anywhere. Thus a unique dimension is exemplified in Hopewell art.

Then, just as rapidly as the Ohio Hopewell culture soared to great heights, so did it disintegrate and fade from view. The cause or causes for the fall are unknown. Speculations run the gamut from plagues, floods, hurricanes, wars, or civil conflicts. The hilltop ramparts suggest the threat of marauding peoples in the region. Some also believe from the evidence of tree rings that a severe drought forced the abandonment of the farming villages. Whatever happened, it is certain that by A.D. 600 the Ohio Hopewell culture came to a rather sudden halt. Many of the arts and crafts were either forgotten or survived imperfectly. Effigy pipes were never so beautifully carved again. The art of cutting and engraving copper, mica, and bone disappeared. No one remembered how to transform stones and pearls into jewel-like ornaments.

Wherever the Hopewell Indians migrated, as many must have done, they probably merged with other tribes but persisted in making and doing things their own way. Their cultural and artistic imprint, however faint, has been traced in different directions at different times. Those who may have settled in what is now southern Wisconsin continued to construct earthen burial mounds, but in the form of birds and beasts, obviously inspired by the memory of the Great Serpent Mound in southern Ohio. Archaeologists call these Wisconsin aborigines the Effigy Mound Indians, and date their culture from A.D. 700 to 1300. Wisconsin villages were small and scattered, but some of their mounds were enormous. One structure, shaped like a hawk with outstretched wings, measured 624 feet from one wing tip to the other. There were few objects within these burial mounds, and at best these were crude versions of the Ohio carvings. Descendants of these Effigy Mound peoples may be the Menomini, Dakota, and Algonkian tribes, some of whose members still survive today.

Other Hopewell Indian bands moved northeast and settled in upper New York State. Like their Wisconsin cousins, they also merged with the Indians they found living there. Their descendants were probably the Algonkians, whom the early European explorers encountered in the seventeenth century. Among the customs retained by them was the antler-horn headdress worn by priests and chiefs, similar clothing and hair styles worn by villagers, and an almost identical linear decoration used by their artists.

Still another group of Hopewell Indians probably migrated down the Mississippi River, which would be the natural course to take, and injected new life and spirit into the Indian communities that were gradually growing along the Gulf Coast. Mound building reached a final crescendo among these southeastern Indian tribes before being made obsolete by the invading white man.

TEMPLES, CULTS, AND CASTES

Along the southern half of the Mississippi River, there was another Mound Building culture. It was probably born and bred amidst the Hopewell trading outposts. It seems to have expanded rapidly in several directions—eastward into what is now Georgia, westward to Oklahoma, northward into Wisconsin. It may have even reached across the Gulf of Mexico to Yucatan and other parts of Middle America. Because the settlements were dominated by wooden temples atop earthen mounds, archaeologists have given the name of Temple Mound to this culture, and date it from the end of the Ohio Hopewell period to the arrival of the white man, that is from A.D. 700 to A.D. 1600.

These southern Indians perfected a new style of mounds that featured pyramidal, sharply outlined, flat-topped structures crowned with wooden temples for sacrifical and other religious services. Sometimes these mounds were seventy or eighty feet high with bases covering many acres of ground. The Cahokia Mound, in Illinois, rose more than fifty feet from a rectangular base seven hundred feet wide and one thousand feet long. A truly imposing shrine, it covered an area of sixteen acres. It has been estimated that three times the earth used in the embankments of Fort

Ancient, Ohio, was used in building Cahokia. Not only is Cahokia the largest single earthwork in the United States, it also exceeds the acreage of the largest Egyptian pyramid. Like the pyramids along the Nile, it was part of the complex religious and ceremonial activities.

The approach to the summit of Cahokia consists of four terraces or platforms. Most Temple Mounds have stairways or ramps of slanting logs extending up one side toward the summit where the temple stood, usually constructed of mud-daubed wattle made of twigs and flexible branches. To build these temples the Indians pounded upright poles into the earth at the top of the mound. Branches of willow or stalks of cans were woven in and out through the gaps between the poles. This basketlike construction was daubed over, inside and out, with mud. Early French explorers in the region wrote that the dried mud of the walls was painted over with pictures and decorative designs. Unfortunately no painted walls have survived, nor have illustrations of them been found in written records, so only speculations can be made about the appearance of the finished work. Charcoal remains indicate that a fire was kept burning within the temples, perhaps the Eternal Fire that played such an important role in the religious ritual of later Indian tribes such as the Natchez.

Temple Mounds were built in clusters around large central plazas. One can visualize magnificently clad chieftains and priests on the top of the truncated pyramid, directing the assembled crowds of villagers below in the complex rituals that would placate the angry gods, insure abundant harvests, ward off evil spirits, and frighten attacking enemies.

Wars were all too common among these Indians. Villages were therefore surrounded with wooden palisades, remains of which have been found at Etowah in Georgia and Moundville in Alabama. Some palisades were planned with complicated mazelike passageways where attackers could be trapped and destroyed by the defenders stationed on the walls above. Wide ditches or moats in front of the palisades improved the defenses and rendered some villages practically impregnable. The walled towns must have reminded the first European explorers of their own medieval hamlets. Indeed, the great Temple Mounds, soaring above the encircling palisades, might well have recalled the cathedrals of their old towns. Their functions were the same.

The Temple Mound villages were much bigger than the settlements of the Hopewell and Adena Indians and indicated a far more complex society. Archaeologists have unearthed evidence of villages of two hundred to three hundred houses within an area of more than five hundred square feet. Instead of the round Adena and Hopewell house plan, the Temple Mound Indians's houses were rectangular, with wattle-and-daub walls and thatched roofs. One to two thousand, perhaps even more, people inhabited the compact communities.

Life in the Temple Mound towns was sustained primarily by farming the fields that stretched for a considerable distance beyond the palisade walls. The land was cultivated with hoes made of flint and shell and possibly by primitive wooden plows. The traditional crops—corn, beans, squash, pumpkins—were grown, but with improved strains and more abundant crops. The harvested surplus was stored away in ceramic vessels until needed. Fishermen continued to be essential providers of food, augmenting the game that hunters stalked in forests, swamps, and along the river bluffs. All plied the winding rivers in dug-out canoes that facilitated communication and transportation.

Unlike their Burial Mound ancestors, the Temple Mound Indians buried most of their dead in large cemeteries located outside the village area. There were exceptions, however, as some burials have been found beneath the floors of houses or seemingly discarded in refuse pits. Cremation was less commonly practiced by these Indians, but they did use bundle burials, whereby the skeleton was flexed or folded and bones arranged in piles. Sometimes the body had been forced into a pit or into a pottery vessel. The occasional burials made within or beneath the floor of the temple mounds were more carefully constructed stone-lined graves, ap-

parently made with very special care for priests, chieftains, or members of their families. The finest ornaments and carvings have been recovered from these graves.

Many excellently made pottery vessels have been found. Some were decorated with linear patterns that were variations on Hopewell themes; others had two or more looped handles. Some vessels had been painted in combinations of black and white or red and buff colors; some were modeled in the form of animal or human figures. These so called effigy vessels are reminiscent of those made by contemporary Mexican Indians, but they are more crude and clumsy. Effigy smoking pipes were large and often so heavy that a hollow wooden stem had to be inserted into the smoke channel for them to be used. Their angular and blocky style was a far cry from the graceful refinements of the Hopewell pipes. The elbow pipe, shaped much like the pipe of today, an innovation of these Indians, was the direct ancestor of the Grand Calumet, or Peace Pipe. There were stone gorgets, either plain or decorated with geometrical or effigy designs. There were many awls, pins, and personal adornments fashioned from stones, bones, and shells, especially the large conch shells.

Unusual and distinctive masks were made from hammered copper. Although simply shaped, a notable example had a long pointed nose and has been called the "Long-nosed God." Whether it was intended to represent a god, and, if so, what one, or how the mask was used, can only be conjectured. Long-nosed gods were portrayed by Maya artists and the origin of this type mask may have been in Mexico.

Strangely, and quite suddenly, it would seem, the Temple Mound people were seized by a religious revival sometime after 1400. Archaeologists have called it the Death Cult. Death was now more than an obsession. It was a morbid, terrifying fear that gave birth to a new type of art. Crammed into graves with the dead were ferocious, frightening images made of stone, bone, copper, pottery, and shell. There were shell masks with weeping eyes vividly portrayed; there were stone and clay deathheads with sightless eyes and lips bared to reveal protruding teeth. Feathered warriors were represented carrying decapitated heads of their victims; engraved almost everywhere were human bones and grinning skulls, horrible to behold. The macabre designs included hideous spiders and centipedes, eyes superimposed on human hands, swastikas, sunbursts, and weird combinations of human, animal, and serpent forms. Most graphic of all was the flying serpent, surely a relative of the great Mexican feathered serpent god Quetzalcoatl. The winged serpent's sinuous body and his forked tongue protruding from open sharp-pointed beak heightened his ferociousness. Borne across the heavens on giant eagle wings, the monster cast his terrifying shadow over stockaded Indian villages from Georgia to Oklahoma.

Dark, somber rituals must have matched and made use of these frightening images, but these rites are hidden behind the veil of the past as are the causes of this widespread cult. About a century before the Spaniards landed in Mexico, the Death Cult held sway. Its intensity increased when wild rumors announcing the arrival of these newcomers from the east spread rapidly across the Gulf of

Mexico and the Rio Grande. Bearded white strangers there were, carrying weapons that killed like a thunderbolt, riding never-before-seen beasts, and garbed in armor that reflected a dazzling light. The end of the world must have seemed at hand, as it eventually was for the fear-ridden Temple Mound Indians.

When the Spanish Conquistadors finally entered the region with their small but adventurous bands, the temples had fallen into ruin, the mounds were abandoned. Like the Hopewell, the Temple Mound Indians vanished, except for their shadowy presence that has been traced among other later Indian tribes.

In the seventeenth century, Spanish, French, and English colonists in the lower Mississippi Valley cohabited with about thirty thousand Indians distributed in about fifty large towns. The Indians were loosely bound into a sort of tribal confederacy. The most powerful tribe called themselves the Muskhogean. English traders later changed the name to Creek after the Ochigee Creek along which their villages were located. They have been known as Creek ever since. Their language, Muskhogean, was commonly spoken by other Indians although they were not necessarily related to each other. There were the Chickasaw who lived near Memphis; the Choctaw who were scattered southward along the Gulf Coast; the Cherokee, one of the largest tribes of all, who lived north of the Creeks. All of the Muskhogean tribes hunted and farmed in Temple Mound territory; some even lived close to the mounds, but none of them seemed to know of the ancient builders. Inspired by these imposing earth structures, some tribes attempted to build their own mounds, but succeeded only in erecting much smaller ones upon which their chieftains' houses might be constructed.

From their European neighbors have come accounts of the games played by these Indians of the Temple Mound culture. English traders watched the popular game that they called Chunky. It was played by two Indians with eight-foot poles sharpened at the ends. After one Indian rolled the chunky—a round stone about five inches in radius—down the field two players running abreast hurled their poles, like javelins, at it. The player whose stick landed closer to the stone when it stopped rolling scored a point, and if his stick touched the stone he tallied two points. The game was played for long periods by Indians who gambled recklessly on the outcome. Some would bet whatever they owned—clothing, weapons, houses, and even their women.

Lacrosse, named by the French settlers, was another very popular game. It was played on a five-hundred-foot field by teams of sixty or more Indians, each equipped with a stout stick with a basket of leather thongs tied at one end. The object of the game was to scoop up a leather ball with the stick, run downfield dodging through the opposing team, and throw the ball through their goalposts. Twenty goals was the winning score. This was a bruising game with hardly any rules, and it produced many broken arms, legs, and even necks.

European observers recorded the corn harvest or "busk" ceremony, probably an outgrowth of the Death Cult. This was a four-to-eight-day festival that marked the first gathering of the corn and the beginning of the new year. Homes and plazas were swept clean and sprinkled with fresh sand; fires were extinguished; all crimes except murder were forgiven; new laws were adopted; dancing and games continued well into the night.

To mark the end of the old year, bodies were cleansed by fasting and swallowing a horrible black drink made from the leaves of a shrub, ilex cassie, which induced vomiting and sometimes serious convulsions. When the ceremonies ended, new fires were lighted, and the life of the village returned to normal as the Indians embarked upon a new year.

Most interesting of all the Muskhogean were the Natchez, apparently direct descendants of the Temple Mound culture. Many of their attitudes and beliefs may be reflections of a cultural tradition extending far back to the past. The Natchez Indians lived in nine or more villages grouped around the great Emerald Temple Mound just east of what is now Natchez, Mississippi. Limited in numbers to not more than four thousand tribesmen, they alone are known to have had a king who was absolute monarch over the tribe. Known as the Great Sun, the king was also a high priest and was believed to have descended from the sun god. He controlled the lives and property of his people, except in military matters when he was governed by a council of old men. As among most primitive people, the aged were accredited with great power and wisdom.

The Great Sun and his wife, Woman Sun, lived in a large house built at the summit of a flat-topped earthen mound. Local retainers attended the Eternal Fire burning within the symbol of his power, the sacred temple, built on a nearby mound. The bones of precious kings were stored there. Only the Great Sun and his chosen priest could enter this temple. An important function of the Great Sun was performed each morning. Upon arising at daybreak, he would ascend the temple mound, point to the rising sun, and indicate its course across the heavens.

So sacred was the Great Sun that he could not defile himself by setting his feet upon the ground. He had to be carried about on a litter elaborately adorned with goose feathers, cushioned and heaped with buffalo robes, bear skins, and other furs. When it was necessary for him to walk, mats were spread in his path. Clad in a feathered cloak, with a crown of swan feathers, tattooed from head to feet, he was a magnificent Indian version of King Louis XIV, the Sun King who ruled France and controlled much of Europe at this time.

The Natchez Indians, like the people of seventeenth-century France, were divided into two classes, the aristocracy and the common people. Beneath the Great Sun the aristocracy was made up of the nobles and the honorables. Beneath them were the masses of common people known as Stinkards. Although badly treated by aristocracy, the masses did command some respect. The word "stinkard" could not be mentioned in their presence by aristocracy as it was too offensive. Unlike the French aristocracy, the Natchez nobles were forbidden to intermarry, but had to select their wives or husbands from the stinkards.

The intermixture of upper and lower classes was but one unique feature of Natchez society; the other was the extraordinary power vested in the female. The woman dominated her husband, regardless of class, and owned property and house. She alone gave rank to their child. Because of this, Natchez society had an unusual pattern. Children of the female Sun were automatically granted the rank of Suns; children of female nobles were nobles; and those born of an honorable woman were likewise honorable. As children of the feminine noble wedded to a stinkard rose in the social scale, the children of the male and his stinkard wife were degraded in rank. Sons born to the great Sun King fell one another to the rank of nobles; sons of noblemen were reduced to honorables; and sons of honorables became stinkards. Children of stinkard parents remained stinkards and often had the privilege of marrying whom they pleased.

The female, whether Sun, noble, or honorable, selected her mate from the stinkard class. When a male stinkard married a female Sun, he became the Great Sun himself, with all the privileges and duties accorded that position. But the wife, the female Sun, as often happened in the courts of France, was the power behind the scenes. Although her husband, the Great Sun, directed the awesome ceremonies of the village, when in the presence if his wife he had to stand like a servant and praise her every word however ridiculous it may have been. He was forbidden to eat with her, and he could even be evicted from the house or have his head chopped off for a major offense. At her death he was killed to accompany her. He had no power at home, but his children could become Suns.

This exalted position of women was not unique to the Natchez. It has been recorded among other tribes, such as the Iroquois and the Pueblos of the Southwest. It may have resulted from the economy and practices of an agricultural people where the growth of crops was vital, and where women did most of the work in the fields. Whether this system prevailed among the Mound Builders will never be known for certain. More than likely, some sort of class system must have existed from very early times; even an absolute monarchy is possible.

After years of cordial coexistence with their French neighbors, minor skirmishes erupted and soon mushroomed into an all-out attack by the Natchez Indians upon the white men. In the first of many Indian wars, the Natchez tribe was defeated by the metal,

gunpowder, and cavalry of the French. Eventually they were almost completely exterminated. Only the city on the banks of the Mississippi has survived to perpetuate the name.

What was the fate of the other Indian tribes in the region? The

Cherokees, Chickasaws, Choctaws, and Creeks formed an alliance among themselves and with the white settlers. When the Seminoles joined them, they were called the Five Civilized Tribes. These Indians shifted their support from one European power to another as conditions changed. They successfully played the dangerous game of power politics until the Revolutionary War, when they misjudged the situation and sided with the British. When the defeated English forces withdrew, the Indians were left to face the wrath and revenge of the new American colonists, who ruthlessly overran and appropriated their lands. Through a combination of force, fraud, and liquor, plus an act of Congress in 1830 that legalized the confiscation of all Indian lands east of the Mississippi, the Temple Mound culture was shattered. The Seminoles resisted and retreated to the swamps of the Florida Everglades. Through hide-and-seek maneuvers, courage, and sacrifice they staved off all efforts of the American government to remove them. The three-year war that they waged cost fifteen hundred American troops and twenty million dollars in military expenses. Undefeated, the Seminoles finally made peace on honorable terms. Many of them left the swamps. Some remained behind in the Everglades and are still there.

The Five Civilized Tribes, or what remained of them, were moved and given grants of land in Oklahoma that would endure, promised President Jackson, "as long as the grass grows and the water runs." Herded and pushed relentlessly westward, the Indian suffered degradation, despair, and tragedy unparalleled in all his long ancient history. Thousands perished from disease, drowning, and exposure on what Indians called the Trail of Tears.

Like sentinels and symbols of the grandeur of their past, the earthen monuments and palisaded villages silently witnessed the end of the Mound Building Indian culture.

CULTURE BY THE BASKET

Where the Rocky Mountains merge into the vast arid plateau of the Southwest in Arizona, New Mexico, and the neighboring borders of Colorado, Utah, and Texas, in this dry, barren, inhospitable land of deep canyons, dusty deserts, and petrified forests, some of the greatest towns of North America grew up. Some were spectacular cliff dwellings dug into the yawning mouths of towering cliffs; others were built on lofty ledges; still others were in the valleys of erratic rivers.

There are thousands of town sites scattered far and wide across the Southwest. Nearly all of them had been abandoned before the Spanish Conquistadors, flush from their victory over the Aztecs, came into the region seeking gold. About twenty-five cities have survived to the present day, and their inhabitants still perform the ceremonial dances and follow some of the rituals of their ancestors. What they have acquired from modern civilization, they have shaped to their own needs and interests. These towns, and the people that built them, are popularly called Pueblos, a Spanish word having several meanings—town, village, race, nation, populace. Archaeologists more scientifically call these Indians the Anasazi, which is a Navajo word meaning "the old ones." Indeed, the roots of these town dwellers extended far back into the past.

The history of the Anasazi Indians began in the Ice Age more than twenty thousand years ago. The northern reaches of the globe—Europe, Asia, and North America—were covered with huge sheets of ice. Below the glacial line, stretching from Iowa to Long Island, the land was carpeted with grass, flowers, and forests and watered with flowing streams. The warm, wet, verdant Southwest played host to a profuse and varied assortment of animals that lured bands of huntsmen. Bones of mastodons, mammoths, camels, bison, horses, and numerous smaller beasts, which were killed and butchered for food and clothing have been unearthed, but no traces of man—skeleton, bone, or even tooth—have been found. Proof of their presence rests on their skill as weapon makers. The first dramatic discovery of an ancient death-dealing point was made by Dr. J. D. Figgins of the Denver Museum of Natural History. In 1926 he unearthed spear points deeply imbedded in the petrified bones of a bison known to have been extinct on the American continent for twenty thousand years. Because these points were found near Folsom, New Mexico, the early bison hunter is called Folsom Man. A number of his sharp-edged points, distinctly shaped with a narrow groove running vertically up the center, have been found in the Ohio River Valley, where they must have been used by hunters like the primitive bison slayer.

Immediately after the Folsom discovery, archaeologists tracked down traces of other early hunters. Each group or tribe of these early killers made its own style weapon point, and these, like the Folsom point, have been given names derived from the modern sites where they were found. Thus, there is the Sandia hunter named after a cave near Albuquerque and dated before the Folsom, twenty-five thousand years ago. There are the Yuma points from Yuma County, Colorado; the Gypsum Cave points from Nevada; the Clovis points from New Mexico.

These very early hunters of the Southwest, besides sharpening flint heads, had to sharpen their wits and develop teamwork in

Bella Coola
Salish
Nootka
Crow
Sioux
Iroquois
Cheyenne
Comanche
Hopewell
Adena
Basket Maker
Pueblo
Mogollon
Hohokam
Temple
Mound

order to slay their giant prey. They probably attacked the younger and weaker beasts or lured them into swamps or pits where they could be more easily destroyed. With sufficient numbers and enough noise they could have frightened the animals and driven them over a precipice or into narrow mountain passes where they could be maimed by boulders thrown down upon them by hunters stationed above.

About ten thousand years ago, the forces of man and nature combined to wipe out the herds of wild beasts. Improved skills of an ever increasing number of hunters thinned the animal ranks. More devastating was the climatic change that brought drier and warmer weather to the Southwest. The cool, moist, forested habitat of Folsom man was replaced by glaring sun that turned the terrain into arid or semiarid desert. The heat and dryness proved too much for the big furry-skinned animals, and they gradually became extinct. Only the modern breed of bison-buffalo survived the passage of time to be hunted by Indians down to the turn of the twentieth century.

Several thousand years later, a new culture made its debut on the archaeological stage of the Southwest. They were not big-game hunters, but foragers who gathered the wild foods of the desert. Often called Desert Indians, they began to settle in southwestern Arizona while it was still occupied by hunters and by mammoths and camels. Primitive nomads, these desert Indians adapted themselves to the climatic changes and lived by collecting seeds, berries, and roots and by killing such smaller game as rabbits, prairie dogs, and doves. The best known group of desert food gatherers was the Cochise culture, named after a site excavated near the town of Cochise, Arizona, in 1926. Carbon-14 tests on one site prove that they were here before 6000 B.C. Evidence of the Cochise are the heavy, durable miling stones they used to grind the roots and seeds into flour before cooking. The seeds were placed in the hollowed-out center of a large stone slab, called a "metate," and pounded by hand with a round stone "mano." Finds of a few spear points at Cochise sites indicate a declining interest in hunting.

The clever Cochise made the cultural leap forward from foragers to farmers. Maize, or corn, was their staple crop. The first strains of corn, dated about 4000 B.C., were only a few inches long and lacked a husk. The inferior species was gradually improved, and soon greater yields of larger ears were harvested. Because corn could be stored for long periods without spoiling, village life became more stable and secure. Houses were built over shallow pit foundations, supported with wooden poles and roofed with twigs and branches. The Cochise learned to transform the tough fibers of yucca and other desert plants into sandals, mats, nets, and baskets.

Before 300 B.C. the Cochise had learned to make pottery. Whether the craft and art of ceramics came to them from the more advanced civilization of Mexico or was their own invention is a continuing argument among southwestern archaeologists. Whatever the origin of pottery may have been—and there are many theories, such as from mud-smeared baskets, coiled pots, nature-hollowed stones, shells, goards—it provided the Cochise with watertight vessels for carrying the scarce water from distant sources, and it insured safer storage of corn and easier and more efficient cooking and preparation of food. Corn was often stored in stone-lined pits found within the Cochise villages. Sometimes bodies of the dead were also put into these pits, together with offerings of baskets, bags, and nets for the use in life after death.

The Cochise culture spread throughout Arizona and inspired the Anasazi and other Indian tribes of the Southwest. Although the origin of the Anasazi is uncertain, some scholars believe they drifted northward in small groups from Cochise country into the San Juan River Valley. Their first villages and cornfields were small, much like those of the Cochise, but with ingenuity and imagination, stubbornness and stamina, they built the grandest towns of ancient North America.

From the San Juan Valley, the Anasazi spread throughout the region known as the Four Corners—a high mountainous plateau or mesa where the corners of the present states of Arizona, New

Mexico, Utah, and Colorado meet. This is a land of striking contrasts and stunning beauty. The sagebrush-covered mesa is slashed by twisting rivers and deep canyons, eroded terraces and steeply rising mountains, whose sides are clothed with forests of juniper and pinion trees; their peaks are covered with snow all the year around. The rivers that cut through the canyons are for the most part shallow and muddy. Many dry up completely in summer. The spring thaws send torrents of water from the melting snows of the mountaintops rushing down through the canyons; sometimes heavy summer rains suddenly send flash floods racing down the mountain trails. Baked by the steady heat of the sun, the mesa is an arid, formidable terrain with scanty grass, sparse game, and few wild food plants. Here began the Anasazi story more than two thousand years ago. Two main divisions of the civilization are recognized: the Early Basket Maker stage, dated one or more centuries before Christ to about A.D. 700; and the later Pueblo phase, which has no terminal date, for the Pueblo Indians still live in New Mexico and Arizona.

Anasazi culture was fairly primitive in its early days. Like the Cochise, they gathered seeds and fruit in the valley, raised enough corn to survive, sought shelter in mountain caves, and, when caves were not available, they built crude shelters of poles and brush. In shallow pits they stored their surplus food. And sometimes they crammed in bodies of their dead, together with funerary offerings, and covered them over with stone slabs. The protection of the deep cave and the dry climate of the region preserved the flesh and hair of these bodies like embalmed mummies. Unlike Egyptian mummies, which were preserved by artificial substances and special embalming techniques, Basket Maker mummies were dried out and preserved by a happy accident of nature. Baskets found with these mummies for the first time in 1893 were so superbly made that they gave the Indians their modern name. From bodies and baskets, weapons and tools, found in these graves, archaeologists have been able to reconstruct the way these ancient people looked and lived.

The mummies show that the Basket Makers were not so very

different physically from the Pueblos of today. They were short and stocky with brown skins and coarse black hair. None of the mummies were clothed. Apparently the Indians wore little clothing: the men a brief loincloth, and the women a little apron. The scant clothing, especially for the men, was compensated by varied hair styles and ornaments. Some men wore their hair long; others cut the sides and left a mop on the middle of the head, or braided it with a cord as a pigtail in the back. Bone and feather ornaments further enhanced their appearance. Women combed their hair very simply, not from any lack of vanity, but because of necessity. Their husbands periodically cut the tresses short with a sharp stone knife and used the shanks of hair for tying and weaving. Both men and women wore ear ornaments, bracelets, and necklaces strung with beads of stone, bone, seeds, and acorns. Ornaments made of abalone and clivella shells from the Pacific coast testify to some widespread trading.

The Basket Makers made ingenious use of native fibers and materials of varied sorts. String entwined from human hair, plant fibers, and animal fur were woven into nets, coverings, containers, and all manner of objects needed for survival in the hot, harsh environment. Fibers of the yucca and apocyum plants were braided and woven into thick-soled, square-toed sandals essential for walking across this rough, rocky, thorny-plant country. These sandals were often decorated with a fringe of buckskin or shredded juniper bark and tied to the ankles with strings of human hair passed through loops at the heel and toe for security. In the belief that sandals would be needed in the afterworld, a newly made unworn pair was placed beside nearly every mummy. Many mummies were wrapped in shrouds woven from strands of yucca fiber reinforced by strips of rabbit fur. These coverings must have been used before death to provide warmth in the cool evenings and winter months.

At one Basket Maker site, archaeologists found a hair-and-fiber string that, before it had been tied into a net, measured four miles in length. Like a giant tennis net it was 240 feet long, more than 3 feet wide, and weighed 28 pounds. The Indians had strung it

across the mouths of narrow gorges and canyons to trap and ensnare small animals stampeded into it.

Best known of the Basket Maker artifacts are the superb baskets, bowls, and trays deftly woven from strings of yucca fiber. Some baskets were so closely coiled that they were watertight and could be used for cooking. Other baskets, used for carrying water from distant springs, had narrower mouths than the cooking baskets to keep the water from splashing out. Often they were coated inside with resin to make them watertight and were held by handles made of cords of human hair or other fibers. Some of these baskets were decorated with red and black designs in a variety of geometric patterns. These sharp angular patterns seem like abstractions of the rocky terrain of the Four Corners region. Similar colored designs also decorated sandals worn by some of the villagers.

Sometime around A.D. 450 or 500, the Basket Makers abandoned their simple houses of sticks, made in the mouth of caves or on the terraces of mountainsides, for the open mesas. Here they constructed more substantial villages. Archaeologists call this the Modified Basket Maker period. During the next two centuries, the Southwest Indians made considerable cultural progress, climaxed by the building of Pueblo cities.

Basket Maker houses originally rose from circular pit foundations ranging from ten to thirty feet in diameter. The floors were covered with a clay coating that sloped upward to meet the half-buried logs that formed the walls. Above the wall foundations, a series of horizontally stacked timbers inclined inward at the top and were roofed by a layer of logs, brush, and thatch plastered with mud to form a dome. Inside there were storage pits sunk into the floor, fireplaces, and a smoke hole in the roof that might also serve as an entrance to the abode. The roof was only about five feet high, barely high enough to accommodate the short, stocky inhabitants.

Variations and innovations were the keynotes of this period. Villages varied in size from a few to over a hundred houses. The basic pit house plan ranged from the common oval shape to the later rectangular or square shape with rounded corners. Measurements remained the same as before, but instead of wood, stone slabs or a combination of stone slabs and plaster were usually used to line the walls. The roof was supported with more sturdy timbers; the smoke hole was converted into a hatchway through which the inhabitants could enter on a ladder thrust through the opening. The earlier side entrance into the house was now converted to a ventilator for the fireplace and decreased in size.

To prevent the cooking fires from suddenly flaring up when a gust of wind whipped through the ventilator, the Indians set up an upright stone, known as a deflector, between the fireplace and the opening. The deflector also made it easier to enter and leave the house. The main living quarters were improved in some houses by putting the storage pits in a smaller separate room connected to the house. Basket Maker houses, like those of their Adena Indian contemporaries, were bare of furniture. The occupants crouched down to eat and slept on the floor cushioned by blankets.

Indians probably spent little time inside these houses, as they were dark, smoky, and obviously not very comfortable. By the middle of the period, around 600, some Indians devised a flat-topped roof in place of the domed type. Much of the living and household activity took place in the open air on this roof.

Although in the course of time the houses were modified inside and out, one feature remained standard and unchanged in nearly every house. This was a small circular hole on the side of the fire pit opposite the deflector. Usually filled with clean white sand, this hole, known as the "sipapu," represented the place where their ancestors first emerged into this world from the underworld where they were created. Archaeologists know this because the sipapu continued to be made by the Pueblo Indians, and accounted for by the ancient myth.

Improvements in house building kept pace with the advances in agriculture. New varieties of bigger-eared corn were sown and harvested together with other crops. Squash, pumpkins, and cucumbers were planted between the corn stalks so that their wide leaves would shade the tender young corn shoots. Beans, grown in small patches near the house, enriched the Basket Maker diet with needed high protein. Animals and fowl, more easily taken with the innovation of the bow and arrow, were a welcome addition to the menus.

Pottery now appeared in Basket Maker villages. The first pots were thick, clumsy, and brittle. By around 600, Indian women had learned to prepare a more refined clay, tempered with sand, crushed rock, or powdered sherds of vessels that had cracked during firing. The clay was rolled into long strands and built up into the shape desired by the potters. With brushes made from yucca leaves, the ends of which had been chewed until flexible and split, and a vegetable paint probably made by boiling the juice of the beeweed plant, artistic-minded potters decorated their wares. The designs consisted of geometrical forms, not unlike the patterns woven into baskets and sandals. Sometimes simply drawn animal and bird images were portrayed on the vessels.

Baskets and sandals continued to be made with greater skill. The old square-toed type of footware gave way to a more refined scalloped-toed sandal, enhanced with decorative designs in red, yellow, and black cord. Less common, and probably ceremonial in purpose, were small crudely modeled human figures in clay. Corncobs were enhanced with sticks and feathers. There were polished stone disks, stone tubular pipes, and woven medicine bags containing many kinds of small objects. One can do no more than guess at the religious beliefs they symbolized.

With confidence gained from their increasing control over nature, the Basket Makers wearied of living in underground pit houses. They pioneered a more solid and durable style of building community homes. The pueblos of impressive size and complexity came into being.

CITIES IN CANYON AND CAVERN

Architecture was the great achievement of the Anasazi Indians. Widely scattered throughout the canyon country of the Southwest stand the proud ruins of hundreds of pueblos, built at about the same time the great cathedrals rose in European cities. Instead of religious worship, the pueblos served as private residences for Indian farmers and their families. Pueblos differed in size and shape according to their locale and the population they served. Some were constructed on canyon floors, several stories high and terraced. Others were daringly built high above the valley on projecting ledges of rock, or else jammed into deep caverns along the sheer face of cliffs. Pueblos consisted of hundreds of rooms stacked story upon story, which kept pace with the growing population. Unlike in most other cities, it was possible to climb to the terrace of the pueblo and make a circuit of the entire city without ever touching the ground. Once these structures were citadels and crowded cities, now they are deserted melancholy monuments that silently speak of the skill of their ancient master builders.

The multiple-roomed pueblos did not spring up full blown. As with all building peoples, the evolution was gradual. When some Indian groups substituted the pit house of the Basket Makers for above-ground houses linked in rows, the pueblo idea was born. Archaeologists call this the Developmental Pueblo, and they date it 700–1050. This transition period culminated with the cliff dwellings of the Classic Pueblo period, 1050–1300.

Many Developmental Pueblo sites can still be seen in southwestern Colorado, southwestern Utah, and eastern Arizona. These early structures consist of boxlike homes built with adjoining walls and extending in rows from six to fourteen rooms long. The rows were either curved, L-shaped, or U-shaped layouts. As the plans expanded so the materials improved. Walls at first were made of wooden poles plastered over with adobe and sometimes reinforced with stone. This process is often called "jacal construction." The Indians became increasingly proficient in the use of stone and soon built walls of sandstone blocks cemented together with adobe mortar. Upon these solid walls, they erected a second story of rooms. Large wooden beams were incorporated into the structure as roof supports. By 1000, two-storied pueblos became quite common in the Southwest.

These rooms were small and dark, averaged about six by eight feet with ceilings no higher than the height of an upright man. There were no doors or stairs in these compact boxlike rooms. People who lived on the upper story climbed ladders to the roof and entered their house through a trapdoor. Those who lived on the ground-floor rooms made the same approach and descended through the floors of the upper-level rooms to get to their own quarters. Privacy was sacrificed for protection. Indeed, the pueblo was an intimate community—dwelling based on the equality and cooperation of its inhabitants. Signs of skirmish are rarely if ever found among these peaceful peoples.

Archaeologists sometimes call these Developmental Pueblos unit houses, or clan houses, in the belief that they were occupied by single family groups. The society of present-day pueblos is based on clans, a concept that may have an ancient tradition extending back to Developmental days. Descent in these pueblos was traced in the maternal line; thus, a clan consisted of people having the same female ancestor. Houses belonged to women, and the family that lived together included a woman, her daughters, and their families. Husbands belonged to other clans, although they lived with their wives' groups. Men's clans banded together in underground chambers called kivas.

Kiva, a Hopi word meaning "old house," was an exclusive men's club used often as we use our churches today—as a religious and social center. Here took place the preparation and performance of the sacred religious ceremonies of the village, council meetings, club business, lounging, relaxation, and even work in workrooms. Based on the Basket Maker pit house, the kiva was circular in plan, with stone walls and pilaster supports for the roof through which the men entered. There were encircling benches and a central fireplace complete with ventilator and deflector as in the earlier pit house. The symbolic sipapu was dug into the floor, and in some kivas the walls were painted with images of gods.

Villages usually had more than one kiva. Set apart from the houses, the kiva was hidden from sight with the roof flush with the ground. Its subterranean presence was marked only by the column of smoke rising above the village from hidden fireplaces.

Near the kiva was the refuse heap and graves of the dead. Amid broken pottery and tools, torn textiles, animal bones, dirt and debris, the Indians interred the bodies in a flexed position and accompanied them with offerings of pottery and household goods. Some bodies rested so far beneath tons of debris that they were crushed by the weight. It was not from disrespect for the dead that the graves were made here; rather, it was easier to dig a grave in the soft refuse heap than in the hard-packed earth. But considering the large village population few graves have been found. The whereabouts of the cemeteries is one of the major mysteries of the Developmental Pueblo Indians and even more so of the more congested Classic Pueblo sites.

Life in these villages was sustained by farming. Corn was the staple food, supplemented by beans and squash. These crops were cultivated with hard-pointed digging sticks and crudely flaked flint hoes. Dogs and turkeys were domesticated but apparently not for food. This belief is based on the fact that they were given separate burials complete with mortuary offerings—corn for the turkeys and bones for the dogs. Sometimes miniature pottery vessels were placed in the grave. The dogs may have been pets and watch guards who warned of approaching strangers; while turkey feathers were prized for decoration.

Hunting played an important role in these villages. Bows and arrows with long, sharp barbed points were universally used and brought down bear, buffalo, elk, wolf, mountain sheep, deer, and rabbit, all of which were added to the diet.

Cotton was cultivated for the first time. The Indians perfected new techniques to produce thread that was woven into fabrics with looms. These fabrics were made into light blankets, kilts, breechcloths, and other garments. Sandals and coiled and twilled baskets continued to be made, but pottery grew increasingly important and was used for many purposes for which baskets had formerly been employed.

Developmental pottery was now made with a finer paste mixed with pulverized potsherds. Specialization emerged in pottery making just as it had in house building. Cooking pots were simply made with corrugations on the surface and sometimes with painted designs. It was the ceremonial or nonculinary pottery, however, that was decoratively painted and set the stage for the elaborate, richly painted pottery for which southwestern Indian artists are famous.

In referring to this painted pottery it is customary to mention first the color of the design and then the background color, as for example, black-on-white or red-on-white ware, both of which were common in Developmental Pueblo sites. Designs were derived from textiles and baskets and included parallel lines, zigzags, triangles, checkerboards, interlocking frets, and combinations of straight-line patterns. The hesitant approach and lack of skill indicate an experimental stage in the handling of a new medium, and these early vessels can easily be distinguished from those of later periods. After

1000, these patterns were played against the colorful tapestry of Classic Pueblo culture.

The spectacular cities of the Classic Pueblo period are found in three main centers: Mesa Verde in southwestern Colorado, the Chaco Canyon district in northwestern New Mexico, and the region of Kayenta in northeastern Arizona. From these areas architectural advances reverberated across outlying areas of Utah, Nevada, and as far away as Texas. Abandoned about 1300, these cities have since become ruins. Off the main highways, they are hidden from view and can only be reached by long, dusty, rocky roads and narrow winding mountain paths. Today, they are surrounded by deserted deserts and lifeless canyons. But when they were built the terrain was furrowed with green fields and the hills resounded with the sounds of bustling city life. By 1276, a drought set in; the corn fields shriveled and drifts of hot sands claimed the cities. The villagers moved away, the buildings decayed, and crumbling stone walls were the only sounds in this land of the dead.

Before the drought and devastation, these cities dominated the canyon country of the Southwest. About half of them were built in the valleys and on the mesa tops, while the others were later built as cliff houses as protection from marauding bands of Indians who entered the region. In general plan the pueblos were similar, with a mass of connected rooms numbering anywhere from twenty to a thousand. They varied from one to four stories in height, were often terraced with setbacks, and were built in a variety of plans, usually rectangular, oval, or D-shaped. The setbacks provided a series of ledges against which ladders could be placed. In time of attack these ladders could be withdrawn for safety, the only access being through a trapdoor in the roof. Indians also worked and rested on the setback terraces.

Among the oldest pueblos were those built in Chaco Canyon, New Mexico. The oldest dated wooden beam from these pueblos is 1130. Ruins of a dozen monumental and numerous smaller sites are scattered across the barren sandy canyon floor. Once this arid strip of land, ten miles long and one mile wide, supported a population of many thousands. Traces of ancient irrigation systems and countless pine poles that served as roof beams testify to the land's fertility a thousand years ago. Largest of all was Pueblo Bonito, or "beautiful pueblo," erected between about 919 and 1067. Constructed as a single building in a D-shaped plan close to the canyon wall, it commanded a breathtaking view of the valley. The scale of the pueblo was equally startling. It covered three acres and contained eight hundred rooms stacked in a series of terraces five stories high. The curved wall was more than eight hundred feet long and the straight side measured more than 660 feet. At least twelve hundred people were housed in this structure. In fact, Pueblo Bonito was the largest apartment house in the world until 1882 when the Spanish Flats were built in New York City. While the Spanish Flats have since been demolished to make room for towering skyscrapers, Pueblo Bonito survives in quiet splendor.

Pueblo Bonito, like all other pueblos, grew as the need for space arose. Originally, the structure was a cluster of rooms made of

rough-shaped sandstone slabs cemented with adobe. Open spaces in the wall were filled with rock chips and the whole plastered over with more adobe. As the population grew, rooms were added in curved rows to the left and right until the pueblo took on its crescent-shaped plan.

About 1050, Indian bands from an area north of the San Juan River Valley came to Pueblo Bonito. These newcomers, called Late Bonitos, constructed their own apartments upon the growing mass, and moved in. They practiced more advanced masonry techniques, exemplified by walls made of more evenly shaped stones and with edges so sharply cut that the blocks fitted tightly and little if any filling was needed. Great beams stripped of bark supported the tiers of rooms. Smaller poles were placed across them at right angles and covered in turn with mats of peeled willow and cedar splints. A thick coating of earth overlay the whole, forming a floor for the room above as well as a roof for the one below. Rooms of these newcomers averaged about eight by ten feet, with ceilings no more than eight feet high, and were devoid of furniture. Though dark and dismal, they served primarily as sleeping quarters and were seldom used during the day, as most of the life was spent on roof setbacks and in the central plaza.

Most of the kivas were dug into the central plaza, but others were incorporated into the building itself. Distinctive of Pueblo Bonito and several other sites in Chaco Canyon were several huge kivas measuring between forty and sixty-five feet in diameter. Known as Great Kivas, these structures may have served the religious demands of the entire community. The Indians had only stone tools to quarry and shape the stone and a trained eye to determine the sides and corners of the monument. Though lines and angles are not true, their unevenness reveals the human imprint of these ancient builders.

Among the other outstanding structures in Chaco Canyon was Chettro Ketl, dated 1030–1116. This pueblo was also built in a D-shaped plan, but with a masonry technique superior to that of Pueblo Bonito. It contained over five hundred rooms. The front wall was enhanced with a decorative stone colonnade, and beneath the central plaza was an enormous kiva sixty feet in diameter. Pueblo del Arroyo, one quarter mile west of Chaco, was also D-shaped in plan. Built 1052–1117, it had 284 rooms and 17 kivas.

While Chaco Canyon was distinguished by enormous surface pueblos, Mesa Verde was famed for fantastic cliff dwellings. This green table land, fifty-six miles west of Durango in southwestern Colorado, stretches fifteen miles long and eight miles wide and towers eighteen hundred feet above the surrounding terrain. Its walls are gashed with rugged canyons that bite deep into its heart, and its summit is crowned with a heavy growth of juniper and pinion trees. Now converted into a National Park, Mesa Verde during its heyday played host to the whole gamut of pueblo architecture from early pit houses to cliff dwellings.

The greatest of all dwellings along the walls of the canyon is Cliff Palace, first discovered in 1882 by two cowboys in search of wandering cattle. The pueblo fills a huge cavern three hundred feet long by one hundred feet high. Protected by a massive sandstone overhang and open to the sun, the pueblo hovers two hundred feet above the canyon floor. This castle in the sky was built in a series of terraces that rose four stories high, contained three hundred rooms and twenty-three kivas, and housed more than five hundred people. Four tall square towers and a round tower made of carefully curved blocks dominate the structure. There are doorways at one side but no windows. Although these towers are prominent in plan, their purpose is unknown. They may have been lookout towers, fortresses, solar observatories, ceremonial structures; they may have served one or more of these needs, or another yet to be discovered.

Walls of the Cliff Palace were thinner than those in Chaco Canyon pueblos. The architecture was distinguished by the use of loaf-like stone blocks, laid up with little mortar and no center fill. The pueblo so conformed to the shape of the cavern that the side and rear walls of the building were braced against the living rock. Rooms were irregularly shaped, averaged a compact six by eight feet, and seldom exceeded five feet in height. Some rooms were used for the storage of grain, seeds, tools, and milling stones in case of future famine or siege. The living quarters afforded barely enough space for inhabitants to sprawl out on the floor. Most rooms had the traditional trapdoor entrance in the roof; others had narrow doors and windows, but they were so highly placed that they could only be reached by ladder. A unique characteristic of the doorways was a T-shaped design with a wider opening at the upper end than at the bottom. A fireplace provided warmth in many of these cramped quarters, despite the discomfort of poor ventilation. Some families enhanced their living rooms with neatly plastered walls and decoratively painted designs.

An open plaza, twenty by a hundred feet, was the center of village life. Most kivas were found here, although others were made in the rear of the cavern. When not in the kivas, the men worked in the fields and hunted on the mesa top. To get in and out of this penthouse pueblo, they cut niches in the rock face for handholds and footholds. The hardy Indians often climbed these perilous but practical stairways with food and game across their shoulders and jugs of water balanced on their head.

The mesa top was the quarry, and stone building blocks for the pueblo had to be lowered by rope over the cliff face to the cavern floor. Fear of invasion encouraged this extraordinary effort. But it was not the depredation of man, rather the devastation of nature, that finally forced the inhabitants to abandon this picturesque, inconvenient, almost impregnable site not long after it had been finished.

Another well-known cliff dwelling was Spruce Tree House, with 114 rooms, 18 kivas, and the surprising signs of fingerprints left by the builders in the mortar plastered in many places. Smaller but more remarkable was Balcony House, named after the wooden balcony of an upper-story room where the occupants worked and enjoyed the fresh air and spectacular view. This pueblo was hung like a swallow's nest seven hundred feet above the valley and could only be reached by maneuvering across the almost vertical cliff face that led into a narrow rocky passageway. Apparently built here because of a natural running stream at the rear of the cavern, it attracted Indians from neighboring pueblos especially in time of drought. To protect this resource, the inhabitants of Balcony House erected a lookout post and put stone obstructions along the passageway, so that a single Indian could easily hold off the attacks of many.

Fear of drought led the Indians to construct with great ingenuity an enormous reservoir on the mesa that could contain one-half million gallons of water. A series of ditches carried water from this reservoir to Spruce Tree House, four miles away, and probably to Cliff Palace, another mile and a half farther on.

One of the most interesting pueblos of all was so-called Aztec Pueblo, sixty miles to the northeast of Chaco Canyon and just outside of Aztec, New Mexico. The pueblo was named in the nineteenth century by white settlers who believed that the ruins were the work of the Aztecs of Mexico. This pueblo was first planned and built by a group or groups of Indians who had abandoned Chaco Canyon. Like the Chaco pueblos, this structure was well planned in U-shape around a central plaza, three stories high in some places and constructed in Chaco style, of neatly dressed slabs of stone. Then, shortly after it had been completed, about 1124, it was abandoned for reasons unknown.

For a long time the pueblo remained deserted, until a group of Mesa Verde people arrived and took possession. These Indians preferred smaller rooms with lower ceilings that could be entered through their unique T-shaped doorways. Older rooms were therefore partitioned off and new ones were built. Their masonry style was so inferior that it can be easily distinguished from the excellence of the former occupants. The newcomers introduced keyhole-shaped kivas and a most unusual religious structure. Found a few hundred feet behind the main ruin, this curious triwall structure was sixty-four feet in diameter with massive seven-foot walls arranged in three concentric rings. These walls were partitioned into small rooms, eight along the inner circle and fourteen along the outer ring, with the main kiva in the heart of the plan. How the structure and rooms were used is not known, but some archaeologists suspect the building was influenced by contemporary Mexican civilizations and probably commemorated the Quetzalcoatl cult of the Aztecs. Several other triwall structures have been found elsewhere in the Southwest.

West of Mesa Verde and Chaco Canyon is Kayenta, Arizona, the third cultural center of the Anasazi builders. Although a number of large pueblos were constructed in this almost inaccessible region, they were generally architecturally inferior. Keet Seel is one of the biggest, a sprawling city of more than 250 ground-floor rooms, built within an enormous open cliff about 1255–1284. Eleven miles away is Betatakin, built about 1260–1277. This pueblo contained one hundred and fifty rooms and was constructed on the sloping floor of a great cave in a sheer five-hundred-foot sandstone cliff.

The masonry of these pueblos was obviously poor and hastily formed. Stones were irregularly shaped, courses were inaccurate, and the whole was covered with great quantities of adobe mortar. In their rush to finish, the builders frequently reverted back to primitive wattlework walls made of upright poles interwoven with smaller sticks. These structures were indeed a symbolic shell of former architectural greatness.

The most distinctive feature of these Kayenta pueblos was the new-shaped kiva. Instead of the traditional circular underground chamber, these kivas were square, above-ground rooms. Called "kihus," they were entered through a door; but their interiors retained the characteristic fire pit and deflector and probably served the ancient religious rituals.

Although best known for their architecture, the Anasazi also developed a significant material culture. Cotton fabrics steadily increased in importance. They were woven on a loom and were often decorated with colored yarns. Coiled and twined sandals and baskets were still made but with less decoration than those of earlier basket makers. Twilled mats of rushes and leaves were made in quantity and widely used as floor and roof coverings. There were also tubular pipes of clay and stone, beads and ornaments of stone and olivella shell, and pendants of the same materials. Turquoise, however, was the most highly prized material and was reserved for the finest ornaments. From this beautiful blue stone the Indians made handsome mosaics and beaded necklaces.

The Anasazi, however, displayed little interest in sculpture. The tremendous effort of building monumental pueblos seems to have left little energy for the carving of human or animal images. Painted pottery was the art in which the Anasazi excelled. Archaeologists are particularly grateful for this, because pottery is almost indestructible and from the distinctive style of making and decorating pottery they have been able to identify and trace the movements of peoples across the Southwest.

The motifs and design patterns mirrored the landscape of this canyon country. Jagged mountains formed by irregular walls, projecting ledges and deep caverns, and canyons sliced by narrow twisting rivers found expression in the angular and undulating abstract patterns painted on the pottery. Fantastic rock formations vividly framed against clear skies were indeed symbolized in the black-on-white style of painting.

Just as the pueblos differed in shape and form, so did the pottery made by the inhabitants. Chaco Canyon pottery consisted of bowls, pitchers, cylindrical vases, and even human effigies. The main wares were characterized by black-on-white designs strongly outlined in sharp-pointed, angular patterns filled with thin, closely spaced parallel lines. Some red pottery has also been found in this region.

Mesa Verde pottery usually had thicker walls and rims that tended to be square and flat. Although it also used the black-on-white decorations as in the Chaco wares, the motifs and surface finish differed. The angular designs were more uneven than those applied by Chaco artists. Band patterns were common, as were larger solid black areas and occasional life-forms in the designs. Many vessels were highly polished to a glossy surface that sometimes gives an impression of translucence. The most distinctive forms were kiva jars, which resemble flattened spheres with fitted covers resting on an inner rim, much like modern sugar bowls.

Kayenta pottery, in contrast to their inferior masonry, was often excellent in execution. Although it was also black on white, there was greater variety of motifs, primarily interlocking keys, frets, and spirals. Black patterns were often elaborate and so closely spaced that little of the white background remained. Sometimes a negative design resulted, giving the impression of a weblike white design on a black background. Most distinctive of Kayenta pottery were the polychrome wares with base color of orange or yellow and designs applied in black, red, and white. Motifs were often wide broad bands, or groups of geometric and other designs.

The severe drought that struck the Southwest, beginning

about 1276, grew so intense over the next twenty years that the Anasazi were forced to abandon pueblos in Chaco Canyon, Mesa Verde, and Kayenta. They may have been hastened on their way by the stepped-up raids of nomadic warriors, internal discord, and possibly other reasons hidden behind the veil of the past. As they retreated, the Anasazi banded together in the more confined territory of the Little Colorado and Rio Grande Valleys, and here they began a new way of life.

The centuries (1300–1700) that followed the Classic Pueblo era were once considered centuries of decline and were called Regressive Pueblo. Archaeologists have since learned that this was a dynamic period marked by impressive cities; some scholars have renamed it Pueblo Renaissance.

After abandoning the pueblos and moving southward, some Anasazi restlessly retraced their steps northward about 1400. One of these bands were the Hopi, who returned and stayed on the high rocky mesas in northeastern Arizona. Hopi is derived from the name they gave to themselves, Hopitu, which means "peaceful ones." Like those of their ancestors, Hopi pueblos, such as Oraibu, Sungopovi, Walpi, and Awatobi, were built of adobe-covered stone blocks and arranged around a central plaza. Unlike the circular kivas of old, Hopi kivas were rectangular with stone-paved floor, but with traditional fire pit, deflector, and sipapu. Murals painted on the walls of the kivas were backgrounds for their religious ceremonies. Abstract images of animals, birds, feathers, clouds, scrolls, painted in red, yellow, and white, were combined in a complex design whose meaning remains elusive. Applied directly to the stone walls, the water colors soon deteriorated, and new murals were painted over the old. Some kivas had a series of fifteen superimposed layers, and at Kuaua archaeologists counted twenty-nine layers.

Rumors of Anasazi settlements along the Arizona and New Mexico border reached the ears of the Conquistadors in Mexico and evoked images in their minds of the legendary Seven Cities of Cibola. How disappointed the Spanish gold seekers must have been when they arrived and found only the drab adobe walls of Indian pueblos! All these pueblos have now fallen into ruin. On the foundations of an older pueblo, the descendants built, in 1695, the Zuni Pueblo, a favorite stop for visitors today.

While the architecture of the Zuni is like that of their Hopi neighbors, the pottery was uniquely decorated with translucent glazes in black-on-white and green-on-white patterns. These rich glazes spread throughout the Rio Grande region where they were adopted by other Pueblo potters.

Most Anasazi Indians lived within the confines of the Rio Grande extending from Taos to the Mexican border. Scores of pueblos arose across this several-hundred-mile region. Typical of the region was Tyuonyi Pueblo, built between 1383 and 1513 in Frijoles Canyon, not far from Santa Fe. This was a large pueblo two stories high, and in some places three stories high, with four hundred rooms arranged around a central plaza. Distinctive of the site was the importance given to weaving in the men's kivas. Pecos Pueblo, situated along the Pecos River, was among the largest and strongest of all pueblos. Rectangular in plan, it was built in a series of terraces four stories high and housed thousands of people from the time it was completed, about 1300, until the eighteenth century, when it was abandoned. Raids by the Comanche Indians gradually reduced the population of Pecos, and a smallpox epidemic of 1788 practically wiped out all the inhabitants.

It was not disease to which all pueblos succumbed, but to the Conquistadors who rode out of Mexico across the Southwest. First came Coronado, who rode as far north as Kansas in search of gold and glory before withdrawing in despair to Mexico in 1542. Other Spanish expeditions soon arrived, and in 1598, the southwestern territory was made a part of the Spanish Empire. Indians were subjected by the sword and the cross. The military brutally quelled any resistance, while missionaries sought converts and repressed tribal rituals. Indians were decimated by European diseases and raids by mounted Comanches, Utes, Navahos, and Apaches. Despite the combined attacks by the white man, Indians, and nature, Taos and other pueblos revolted in 1680; they captured Santa Fe and held it for the next twelve years. They weathered attacks by Spanish troops and nomadic tribes, but they could not survive the attack of the most feared enemy of all—drought. Just as their ancestors were forced to abandon the great cities to the north, so did these rebellious descendants surrender Santa Fe four hundred years later.

Meanwhile, the Navaho and Apache gained a foothold in the Southwest. They wandered into pueblo country after A.D. 500 from their homes in Canada and Alaska. They harassed and threatened the pueblos with horses acquired from the Spaniards. Uninterested in herding or farming, the Apache lived by hunting and raiding. They lived in a simple pole-and-branch-covered dwelling called a wickiup, which could be put up and dismantled in a matter of minutes. Until they were subdued by the army, the Apache, especially when led by Geronimo, were the scourge of the Southwest.

The Navaho learned from their neighbors and became skillful farmers, and later great herders. They adopted some of the Anasazi religious ideas and excelled in weaving, pottery, silverwork, and sand painting. Navaho pole-and-earth covered dwellings, known as hogans, were like a combination tepee and earth lodge. Subdued by army troops after they had attacked wagon trains, the Navaho were retired to a reservation in northeastern Arizona. But here they made a remarkable comeback; they prospered and increased, and today they number more than eighty thousand.

With hostilities at an end, peaceful coexistence prevailed among the Indian tribes and white settlers. The face of the Southwest, altered by large farms, ranches, towns, and cities, came within the orbit of the modern age. Many Indians entered and were absorbed by the white man's society; others retreated to their pueblos and clung to ancient ways and customs. The Zuni and Hopi still petition their rain gods. In one ceremony they impersonate kachinas, supernatural beings who act as intermediaries between man and god. To attract the kachinas to the village, the men paint their bodies in many colors, wear weird costumes, and cover their faces

with terrifying masks. As they perform the dances and rituals, they look as nightmarish and supernatural as the gods they are supposed to represent. To instruct the children of the village in the more than one hundred kachinas, small doll-like images of each are carved from cottonwood and richly painted and ornamented.

Some Navaho ceremonies resemble circus acts. In purification rituals men thrust flaming sticks into their mouths, walk on burning coals, and cover their bodies with the coals. Other Indians insert wooden arrows down their throats in the belief that they will bring winter rain. The most arresting ceremony is the Hopi snake ceremony, popularly called the Snake Dance.

This is a sixteen-day ritual, performed in late summer when rain is needed for the parched fields, and it involves two secret societies. While one group of men prays in the kiva, the other searches for snakes in the desert. Snakes symbolize lightning to the Hopi Indians. About a hundred or more snakes, both harmless and deadly, are brought back to the village, washed, fed, and lulled by song. The actual Snake Dance is held on the last day. With painted faces and bodies, men hold a snake between their teeth and carry them in their hands as they dance around the plaza. Sometimes the dancers are bitten by the venomous rattlesnake, but they never once lose step or rhythm, nor are any known to have died. After the dance, the men gather up as many snakes as they can carry, rush out of the village, and release them to carry the prayers for rain via the underworld up to heaven.

Painted deserts, rugged mountains, lofty mesas, and deep canyons cut by temperamental rivers, make the Southwest perhaps the most picturesque region of America. Nowhere else in our country can one experience a greater feeling of antiquity, marvelously preserved by the dry climate. For centuries the Southwest challenged the courage, endurance, and ingenuity of the Indian, but he survived and endured conquest and famine, drought and disease, the coming of the white man and attacks of Indian enemies. Despite the odds against him, he cultivated the soil, built unique homes and towns, constructed irrigation systems, and perfected the arts of basketry, weaving, painting, carving, jewelry and pottery making. During this long history there were many tribes, each making its own special contribution to the brilliant mosaic of the Southwest.

VILLAGES OF CEDAR AND SALMON

The jagged coastline from Alaska to northern California played host to a third great Indian culture, which ranked with the Pueblos of the Southwest and the Temple Mound peoples of the Southeast. Indians of the Northwest were unique in their cultural achievements without the benefit of agriculture, pottery making, stone carving, domesticated animals, or heritage and inspiration from other civilizations. From the forests and the sea they formed the foundation for their considerable cultural development. Little is known of their past, but their civilization reached its zenith after contact with Europeans in the eighteenth century. With the white man's firearms, steel knives and tools, clothing and other goods, the Indians of the Northwest flourished, but the cultural flame burned brightly for less than one hundred and fifty years. By 1900, the flame flickered and died as the natives were overwhelmed by sickness, disease, alcohol, and tribal disintegration brought by traders and settlers.

Northwest Indian culture grew up along the narrow twelve-hundred-mile-long coastline, slashed by fiords and spotted with mist-shrouded offshore islands. Villages of gabled cedar-plank houses dwarfed by towering totem poles stood on banks high above the shore, or on narrow beaches of sand snuggled between outthrusting rocks. Battered by wind and rain, these villages clung tenaciously to the exposed coast, framed against thick, dark evergreen forests that rose to the snow-capped peaks of the coastal Rocky Mountains. With overland trails blocked by the almost impenetrable rocky terrain, the canoe was the only means of communication between the clustered villages scattered along the coast. Hemmed in by mountains and sea, Indians of the Northwest indeed created a coast culture.

This culture was composed of seven tribal groups, each of which spoke a different language. Beginning in the far north were the Tlingit, who inhabited the area from the Malaspina Glacier south to the Portland Inlet including most of the Alaskan panhandle. The Haida occupied the Queen Charlotte Islands, the Tsimshian were found along the coast of British Columbia; the Kwakiutl was centered in the area around north Vancouver and the adjacent mainland; the Bella Coola Indians lived on both sides of the Salish River; the Nootka held about half of Vancouver Island and part of Washington; while the Coast Salish occupied the region north of the Fraser River southward down the Washington coast. Although languages were unintelligible from tribe to tribe, in the course of time they traded, borrowed, and shared many forms, customs, and ideas. Certain differences can be recognized in tribal art styles and social expressions, but so much of their way of life was similar, that these tribal groups can be spoken of as Indians of the Northwest Coast.

The origin of these Indians is not known. More than likely, their ancestors migrated into Alaska from Siberia via the Bering Strait more than ten thousand years ago. In small bands they followed the gorges of the Columbia and Mackenzie Rivers southward along the coast. There is little archaeological evidence of their presence. Fragments of wood, horn, bone, and superbly woven sandals from one campsite—Fort Rock Cave in central Oregon—have been dated by carbon-14 about 7000 B.C. Little is known of this period and the many centuries that followed, as most materials have decayed and disappeared in the damp climate of the Northwest. There was some iron, apparently obtained from Siberian Iron Age cultures, fishing and hunting techniques learned from the Eskimos, and certain traits possibly derived from Indian tribes who inhabited the plateau country to the east. Controversy rages over the time and nature of these influences, but there is no question that while these peripheral peoples remained fairly primitive, the Northwest Coast Indians made remarkable cultural progress. Their colorful, complex society developed in relative isolation from any other civilization.

Knowledge of their existence came two hundred years after the Pueblo and Mound Building regions had been penetrated by European explorers. The first to come was Vitus Bering, after whom the Bering Strait was named. In 1741, Bering led a Russian scientific expedition to the Alaskan mainland, but on the return journey he was shipwrecked and died of scurvy on the Komandorskie Islands. Survivors of his crew pieced together a boat and sailed back to Asia, bringing with them lustrous sea-otter furs. More highly prized than sable, these pelts sparked the establishment of Russian trading bases from Sitka, Alaska, down the coast to Mexico.

As the Russians moved south, Spanish ships sailed north from California and touched on Vancouver Island in 1774; four years later the sails of two English ships, commanded by Captain James Cook, hove into view. In his vain search for the Northwest Passage, Cook landed at Nootka to repair his ships, the *Resolution* and the *Discovery*. Greeted by friendly Indians, he and his crew bartered for skins, furs, and sea-otter pelts. In return, the Indians went wild for metal of all and any kind—buttons, doorknobs, cups, and hinges—which they removed from many of the ships' chests. Cook described many of the things that he saw—the richly carved masks, slave girls, different kinds of fish and game, bags of colored ochre, and a horrible dish of roasted human arms and hands served by his Indian hosts.

With his ships repaired, and furs stored in the hold, Cook returned to Hawaii, where he was killed in 1779. His party sailed across the Pacific and traded with the Chinese Mandarins in Canton who paid the highest prices for the otter pelts. Sailors in Cook's crew quickly sold out their collection of furs for fabulous prices; one made eight hundred dollars from the Chinese. Stories of these furs rapidly spread, and within ten years over a hundred ships from many countries—Russia, England, America, Spain, Mexico—came to the northwest coast to share in the lucrative fur trade. The trading posts of the North West Company and the Hudson's Bay Company, which merged in 1821, and the interests of John Jacob Astor competed for the rich fur trade in the Northwest.

These trading posts, well-stocked with material goods and vast quantities of liquor, attracted the Indians. As the population of the villages declined, so did the social structure. Some Indians tried to adopt new ways; others later lived on government reservations; many were forced to work for money on terms dictated by the white man. Without immunity to the white man's diseases of measels and smallpox, thousands of Indians were wiped out. The Haida, for instance, numbered about eight thousand in the mid-nineteenth century, but a Canadian census of 1894 listed only six hundred. Before too long the Northwest Indian may disappear entirely; his former greatness recorded only by wood carvings, woven textiles, and other arts and crafts preserved by museums and galleries.

Before the time of trading posts, tribal life on the northwest coast was pleasant. Food was plentiful, the people did not suffer from drought or deep snow, and the forest supplied good materials for clothing and building. In physical appearance the coastal Indians were very much alike. They were tall in stature in the north, averaging about five feet, nine inches, but somewhat shorter in the south. Their skin was a pale brown with a slightly yellow cast; the hair was straight and black; the nose somewhat flat, and the eyes a deep, dark brown. The men in general had more hair than most American Indians—indeed, some wore beards and mustaches. Many tribes deformed their skulls into a long, tapered, sugarloaf

shape, and richly tattoed and painted their bodies. Clothing was kept to the minimum, except for the display of rank or ceremonial authority. They often went barefoot even in snow, and in warm weather the men went naked while the women wore simple bark skirts. In cold and wet weather, robes or capes, often of shredded bark, and a basket hat gave protection. Although animal skins were plentiful, buckskin garments were seldom worn, because in a very wet climate they soaked up water and became slippery and uncomfortable.

Villages hugged the shoreline and faced out to sea. Usually there was a single line of houses, but some villages had two or three rows of houses set about two hundred feet apart. About thirty or more houses made up a village, each large enough to accommodate anywhere from twelve to over one hundred people. Though the villages were small, they could easily house a population of well over a thousand. Houses were larger than the homes of most other Indians of the Americas. One early explorer reported that he had been greeted inside a Nootka house by a crowd of eight hundred people.

Houses varied in size and construction among the different tribes. Basically, however, all had a rectangular framework with roof and walls built of hewn planks. The planks were fastened to thick log pillars with bark cord, or else set into slots cut into the pillars. Such houses could be dismantled easily and the wood could be used to build temporary fishing camps during the spring and summer. Wall planks were at first secured horizontally, but after the Indians obtained nails from the traders, the planks were nailed up vertically. Northern tribes built nearly square houses with gabled roofs that ranged between forty and sixty feet in width. Houses farther to the south were longer and narrower, anywhere from sixty by five hundred feet, with a flat, shedlike roof.

There was a central fire pit inside, and an opening was left in the roof directly above to permit the smoke to escape. The interior was partitioned with woven wooden mats into sections for each family group. Around the walls stretched a wide platform that served as sleeping area and storage closets for belongings. Houses of important people had one or more terraces set back from the central fire pit. The high-ranking man and his family lived within an enclosed quarter of an upper terrace at the rear of the house. Other relatives lived along the sides of the houses, each within his own cubicle. A high post above the roof carried the carved family crest bearing such names as Killer Whale House, Sun House, or Shark House.

In a region famous for huge trees, it is no wonder these Indians were excellent woodworkers and carpenters. They had a variety of tools including knives, adzes, chisels, hammers, drills, and wedges. Before the introduction of metal in the eighteenth century, tools were made of stone, bone, and wood. Sharp-edged blades were made of shell, beaver's incisor tooth, bone, jade, and iron obtained from Siberia or offshore shipwrecks. Surfaces were smoothed with rough stones and finely sanded with tough-textured sharkskin.

Cedar was the favorite wood of carvers. When bone wedges were forced into one end, the wood split easily into wide, straight

planks. The clean, easily worked grain made cedar the most versatile of woods, and it was carved, painted, steamed, bent, fitted, and inlaid with other materials. The Indians learned to form and shape wood into the smallest boxes as well as towering totem poles. The inner bark of the cedar tree was made into baskets and textiles. Cedar was to the Northwest Indian what bamboo was to the Chinese.

These seagoing Indians made excellent canoes. They ranged in size from the one-man dugout, about twelve feet long, to the giant Haida war canoe, fifty feet long and capable of carrying forty men. Canoes were made from trees, usually felled near the water's edge. After the tree had dried out, the interior was shaped with an adze. The interior was hollowed out by building a fire on the upper side of the log and, as the wood burned, chipping out the charred ashes until the desired shape was attained. To stretch the wood for the insertion of seats, the hollow was filled with water and heated with hot stones. Covered with woven mats, the steam softened the wood sufficiently for the pieces to be forced between the gunwales. Finally, the hull was rubbed to glassy smoothness with sandstone and sharkskin abrasive. Canoes of northern tribes often had a raised bow and stern, but further south they had a more graceful high stern and upward sweeping bow. Some scholars believe these southern canoes may have influenced the design of American clipper ships.

While the men perfected the art of woodworking, the women practiced the arts of basketry and weaving. With bark that had been dried and cut into strips, or shredded into fine threads, they made mats and coverings of many kinds. Sometimes wood bark was combined with the wool of the mountain goat and woven on a simple loom into warm blankets. The glory of the weaver's art was the ceremonial blanket woven by the Chilkat Indians, who were members of the Tlingit tribe. It took about one year to weave these blankets from bark and wool. They were decorated with a mystic design of black, yellow, and blue-green colors, which was imbued, so they say, with the power of speech.

Baskets were so expertly woven from spruce root and barks that they could carry water and be used for cooking. Made into a variety of shapes, these baskets, like the textiles, were richly decorated with color obtained from mosses, roots, mud, berries, and tree-bark dyes.

As cedar was the basic material, salmon was the staple food. It has been estimated that each year the approximately fifty thousand Indians of the northwest coast caught eighteen million pounds of salmon, or three million pounds more than the total catch made by commercial and sport fishermen today. During the spring spawning season, an Indian family might catch and store about half a ton of dried salmon for future use, in the same way that Indians of the Southwest might have stored corn. Though villages were sustained by salmon, the life cycle of this fish was a mysterious phenomenon to Indians of the past as it is to scientists today.

Hatched in gravel beds of freshwater rivers, the young salmon, called "parr", found its way downstream to the saltwater sea, where it lived for years. When full grown, the salmon, as if in answer to some instinctive call, fought its way upstream through rapids and over falls until it reached the very same spot in the gravel beds where it had been born. The female then dropped the eggs, and, after they had been fertilized by the male, swirled her tail protectingly over them. When the eggs hatched, the life cycle was renewed, and the newborn parr swam out to sea, while the parents remained behind to be caught by the Indians.

How the salmon found their way upstream is not known. They may have been guided by the sun and certain rock formations and, with delicate sense of smell, nosed out the home stream. Indians believed, however, that the salmon, like all living creatures, was immortal and was reborn in the sea after he sacrificed himself for the tribe. Whatever the answer may be, the salmon was welcomed with colorful Indian ceremonies when it returned to the rivers.

Salmon, halibut, cod, herring, and smelt were caught with fishing gear that was ingenious, complex, and durable. Fencelike weirs directed the fish into traps made of huge baskets. There was netting, stitched in many sizes and shapes, and fishing poles with many different types of hooks. Salmon were taken with harpoons made of a wooden handle and tipped with bone that had been shaped into one or more barbed prongs. Large flat-bodied flounders were easily taken with a pointed stick or by foot. Candlefish, or eulachon, were so oily that when a wick was pulled through the body of the dried fish it burned like a candle. In forays along the beach the Indians gathered vast quantities of mussels, mollusks, oysters, abalone, and crabs.

Sea mammals, such as otters, seals, porpoises, sea lions, and whales, were hunted with canoe and harpoons. Whaling became a specialized skill among the Nootka. The whaler was a man of high rank, usually the chief, who owned the canoe and crew. Before the hunt, the crew sought special powers through the ordeals of starvation, sleeplessness, and magic rituals. The hunt took the canoe far from land, as it followed the whale out to sea for several days. Since the whale weighed as much as seventy tons, the men who paddled these open canoes required considerable courage and skill. The harpoon was made of mussel shells and antler-horn barbs tied to a yew-wood handle. The line of whale sinew and tough roots was about one hundred fathoms long, with skin buoys tied at intervals. Because the harpoon was too heavy to be thrown, the canoe had to sneak up alongside the whale so that the chief could drive the weapon home. The crew skillfully kept the canoe afloat until the whale tired from loss of blood and from dragging the heavy buoyant line. Another canoe then came alongside and a crew member cut the tendons of the whale's flukes with a sharp mussel-shell bladed spear, rendering him helpless. The final death blow was delivered with a harpoon plunged deep into his heart. After the kill, the whale was pulled ashore and put to good use. The meat, blubber, and skin were eaten; intestines made good containers for water and oil; and sinew was cut into harpoon line.

In the tall, lush forests, Indians armed with pikes, bow and arrow, and later firearms, killed deer, bear, and elk; with nets they snared rabbits and birds; and with sticks they dug wild camass roots, clover, inner bark of trees, and also gathered many kinds of acorns and berries. The lack of starch in the diet, plus the need to keep warm in a damp cool climate, may explain their great fondness for grease and oil. Many of them took enthusiastically to planting potatoes and other crops, which were introduced by the European traders.

A prized delicacy was made by whipping a mixture of soapberry, eulachon oil, and cold water into a froth. A strong cheese was made from salmon that had been stored for a long period of time. Food from the sea and forest was cooked, baked, roasted, and broiled in many different ways. About 1900, a Kwakiutl housewife recited one hundred fifty recipes to an anthropologist without coming to the end of her culinary repertoire.

Recreation and war offered some release from hunting and fishing, carving and building. Men and boys played several kinds of sports on the beach. There was a game in which a long stick had to be thrust through a small perforated stone; a hockey game was played by teams that tried to knock a ball across the goal with wooden clubs. Wrestling, tug-of-war, dice, and guessing games were played for hours at a time as the tension mounted among the spectators.

Warfare, rare among American Indians, was waged by the Nootka and other northern tribes abetted by competing foreigners. The reason was geographical. This was one of the few places in North America where the population was crowded between steep, bleak mountains and sea. Indians fought for the few good village and fishing sites along the narrow coast. Weapons included bows and arrows, clubs, spears, and knives of various lengths. The fighters also wore armor. Helmets were made of wood, usually carved into horrifying faces, and the body was protected with wood slats or a cuirass of heavy hide.

Family feuds were more common to Indians of the Northwest. Insults and killings had to be revenged and indemnities in terms of goods had to be paid for the slain man depending upon his rank. Among the warlike northern Indians it was sometimes impossible to agree on the indemnity to be paid when a man of importance was killed. For the good of the group, a chief or noble related to the killer might sacrifice himself. He put on his finest regalia with his highest insignia and performed a stately dance before the enemy. If the enemy had good manners, they waited until he had come close to them before killing him.

Villages were raided for the purpose of capturing slaves. Although they were not needed for economic reasons, slaves were a symbol of the chief's splendor. Ownership of another human being was a concrete, easily demonstrable form of wealth. To display his absolute scorn of his possessions a chief might have a slave killed and buried with the sinking of a new house post, or have the canoe of a visitor dragged up onto the beach over the bodies of slaves especially slaughtered for the purpose. This bloodshed was part of the potlatch, a ceremony interwoven with the complicated ceremonial rituals, religious beliefs, and colorful art traditions of the northwest coast.

POLES, MASKS, AND POTLATCH

Compared to other primitive people, Northwest Coast Indians placed unusual emphasis upon social status. Their societies were divided into chiefs, freemen, and slaves. The majority of the people belonged to the middle group of freemen. Above them was the chief, usually the oldest direct descendant of the original tribal ancestors. The younger brothers were his heirs and stood next to him in rank. All other members of the family line ranged in rank down to the lowest freemen, who was the most distant relative. A person could be raised in rank because of certain skills, such as canoe making, carving, or building. On the other hand, one could be lowered in rank if he brought disfavor to the tribe. Below the freemen were the slaves captured in warfare and raids. Anyone forced into slavery brought disgrace to his family. If his family lived nearby, he was often ransomed and freed. The original home of most slaves, therefore, was usually located a great distance from the tribe where he was kept.

Below the tribal chief were the clan chiefs. Clans consisted of several family groupings, and in the northern tribes—Tlingit, Haida, Tsimshian—clans were united into what anthropologists call "phratries." Clans played a more important role in these northern tribes. They traced their descent through the mother, while tribes to the south traced descent through the father and mother with emphasis on the father line, as in our own society.

Members of both clans and tribes related their origin to a supernatural animal, or totem. Representations of the totem in the form of crests proudly displayed the member's ancient ancestry, much like the coats-of-arms of European nobility. Mythical ancestors of the Haida were the eagle and raven; among the Tsimshian, they were the eagle, wolf, raven, and bear; the wolf and bear were also common to the Tlingit.

With a livelihood based on hunting and fishing, Northwest Coast Indians developed an acute awareness of animals, birds, and fish. Their myths, memorized and recited and passed on from generation to generation, told how Indians were related to certain creatures. According to the myths, when the world began all living things were basically equal except in outward physical appearance. Salmon, it was said, were a race of supernatural human beings who lived beneath the sea. During the spawning season, the salmon-people, dressed in scale and flesh of the fish, swam upstream and sacrificed themselves to the Indians. They could be resurrected in human form beneath the sea if all bones of the fish were carefully put back into the water, according to certain ceremonial rituals. If, however, some bones were carelessly left on land, the salmon-people would be deformed at birth with arms, legs, and other parts of the body missing. When so unappreciated, the salmon might never again return to the river where the tribe lived.

Many legends told of Yetl the Raven, the mythical creator of all things. One day when Yetl was hungry, he dived into the sea and swam to a village where the Indians were fishing. Keeping himself invisible, Yetl removed the fish from the hooks as fast as they were caught, until eventually he himself was caught. He managed to escape, but part of his beak remained stuck on the hook. The fisherman removed it without knowing what it was. One day Yetl returned in human form, found and replaced the fragment of beak, and flew away through the smoke hole in the roof of the fisherman's house. When hungry once more, he assumed the shape of a chief and, with the chief's staff in hand, sat down among the Indians and ate with them. Either disguised as a chief or depicted with a broken beak, he was immortalized on totem poles of the Tlingit and Haida Indians.

Legends emphasized how kindness toward animals might bring rewards to the tribe in time of need. These legends also recorded the origin of clans. There was the ancestor of the Kwakiutl clan who came to earth in the form of an eagle. He turned himself into a human being but could not change his beak into a nose; thus he was portrayed with this beak on tribal masks. The Haida bear clan traced their origin back to a woman who had been captured and taken as wife by the king of bears. She gave birth to a child by him—half human and half bear—before she was rescued by a group of hunters. Artists delighted in carving her human and animal attributes.

When the Indians hunted and fished for these creatures, in a sense they killed their own relatives. This brought on deep feelings of guilt that could only be compensated through friendship and respect for creatures that were not killed. Thus, animals usually adopted as totems—wolf, raven, grizzly bear, killer whale—were not eaten by the Indians. There were reasons for this: wolves ate corpses, ravens feasted on unclean things, grizzly bears and whales killed people, and so on. Creatures selected for totems were apparently regarded as symbols of atonement for those animals killed for food. Reverence for the divine members of these animal species, combined with the pride of descent from them claimed by chiefs and clans, spurred the prolific art production of Northwest Coast Indians.

Animals and the myths surrounding them provided the theme for much of the art. They were represented on an amazing variety of objects, ranging from the smallest charms to the giant poles. Sculptors worked in wood, bone, ivory (tooth of sea lion or incisor of beaver) and argillite, a soft stone that hardens upon exposure to the air. Designs usually conformed to the material from which they were carved, whether it be a box, charm, headdress, rattle, or house front. Some carvings of animals and chiefs were remarkably realistic, but most of the art was abstract in style.

There was feeling for symmetry and a tendency to avoid open spaces in the design. All the space was filled with parts of faces and bodies, as well as cross-hatching and curvilinear lines. Eyes, conventionalized in style, were often used to mark sockets and joints of animal and human figures. A frequent device of Northwest art was seemingly to split the animal in half and cast one half of the body in profile to the left and the other to the right. The body might become almost unrecognizable, the creature identified only by one or more distinguishing features—the big teeth and sharklike fin of the killer whale, the chisel-like teeth and cross-hatched scaly tail of the beaver, the large pointed beak of the raven. Sometimes an almost X-ray image of the animal was portrayed with the interior structure of spine, vertebrae, ribs, joints, and sockets. Designs were outlined with heavy sweeping lines and painted in red, white, brown, and blue-green. These colors were derived from charcoal, lignite, ochres, and eroded copper. Ground on stone mortars, they were mixed with chewed salmon eggs and vegetable juices to create a temperalike paint.

The most spectacular achievement of Northwest Coast art was the totem pole carved from cedar tree trunks. The figures represented on the poles were not actually totems or creatures of veneration. Rather, they were more like heraldic images that proclaimed the owner's legendary descent from mythical animals. They were erected either as status symbols or memorials to the deceased. Best known are the memorial poles carved by the Haida and Tsimshian sculptors. About ninety feet tall, these columns are the largest wood carvings known, and they are of monumental grandeur, surpassing anything produced by wood carvers anywhere in the world.

The totem pole was usually commissioned by the nephew of the deceased and took the male artists of the village many months to

complete. Carved from top to bottom with superimposed creatures and richly painted in contrasting colors, the design on the pole is a bewildering display. The bright wide range of colors was a modern innovation, as earlier poles were more simply painted. Because of the round shape of the pole, and the necessity of showing the whole animal, artists adopted standard postures with a somewhat rigid pattern. Heads extended around most of the pole, legs were bent or folded, paws drooped, and the most important features were exaggerated. The more totems carved, the taller the pole and the greater the prestige of the man commemorated. To set the carved pole upright was a major feat. A deep hole was dug with a wide sloping trench extending to the base of the pole. With wedges, ropes, and much straining of muscle, the pole was slid down the trench and maneuvered into position.

The earliest poles, carved with axes and jade blades, had rougher surfaces than those later carved with iron tools bought from European traders. Totem poles became the vogue in the nineteenth century; the tallest ones were erected between 1840 and 1880, when Indians had acquired great wealth through the fur trade. About six hundred poles stood before 1900, but many have since fallen and decayed in the humid region. In 1938, two hundred were saved by the United States Forest Service program.

Northwest Coast Indians also carved mortuary poles in which the remains of a high-ranking man were placed. His cremated ashes were put into a wood box or coffin and were placed in an opening somewhere near the center of the pole. A third type of pole served as house posts that supported the roof of the dwelling. Between five and fifteen feet high, these posts were richly carved with the owner's totem crests. An unusual variation were those poles erected in front of the house, with an opening cut through for the entrance-way.

Carved and painted wooden masks, in a great variety of forms, were used during the winter festivals when secret societies impersonated mythical beings. Some masks were made to fit the face; others had long appendages added, such as bird beaks several feet long or the movable body and flippers of the killer whale six feet long. Masks used in the Kwakiutl Cannibal Dance represented a mythical bird with a twelve-foot beak that had to be supported by two men. There were double masks, ingeniously carved and equipped with concealed strings that when pulled by the wearer made the eyes roll, parts twirl, and opened up to reveal another masked face within. Northwest Coast masks were often distorted, grotesque, richly painted, and enhanced by the addition of human and animal hair.

Masks were worn by medicine men in ceremonial performances. Their powers were derived directly from supernatural spirits, dreams, visions, and strange experiences or encounters with spirits.

Respected and feared by the villagers, medicine men communicated with the spirit world and could forecast good hunting, cure disease, bring misfortune to enemies, detect crimes, and practice all sorts of witchcraft. Most arresting were Tlingit and Haida medicine men with elaborate costumes, long uncombed hair, bone necklaces, and rattles and bone tubes in hand that blew away sickness and disease.

Secret societies dominated life during the long, bleak months of winter. The nights grew cold, dark came early, the biting north winds soothed the stormy seas, and ghostly whistles in the dense forest announced the approach of the mighty spirits who walked the earth. The clan system was suspended and ordinary life was at a standstill while these supernatural spirits took over. Ceremonies were enacted at night before villagers who gathered together in the huge house. As the flames rose from the fire pit and cast dancing sparks upward through the roof into the blackness of the heavens, the emotions and imagination of the people also soared to new heights. Huddled in the gloom, they watched spellbound the mysterious dramatic dances performed by the secret societies. When the medicine man put on the mask of the spirit, he indeed transformed himself into the "real" spirit, an illusion heightened through deception, trickery, and theatrical devices. He made people appear and disappear through concealed underground passageways. Voices came out of nowhere and everywhere through speaking tubes hidden beneath the floor and in the walls. Wooden puppets of men, animals, and snakes, tied to invisible strings, followed the performers or suddenly flew across the room. Make-believe fights seemed realistic when blood flowed from deep wounds, but actually poured from hidden animal bladders opened at just the precise moment.

The Kwakiutl had the most secret societies and excelled in clever, effective stage devices. They vividly dramatized the mythical spirits who came to instruct the young as well as to reveal all their supernatural powers. Some societies impersonated the feared monster-bird who lived on top of mountain peaks and devoured human flesh, or the double-headed dragon and cannibal spirits who inhabited the forbidding forest. One terrifying dance told the story of a high ranking Kwakiutl Indian who had been kidnapped and embodied with the cannibal spirit. On his return to the village he performed a frenzied dance and was fed human corpses. Actually, they were the bodies of small black bears fitted with a carved human head. After eating, he danced quietly across the room; then, as if seized by the cannibal spirit, he ran into the audience and with his teeth tore off pieces of flesh from the arms of several spectators. Finally, he was subdued, pacified and enabled to return to normal life.

Dramatic ceremonies marked the initiation of a young boy into one secret society. When chosen for membership, the youth was kept in seclusion and taught the ways, rituals, dances, and songs of the society. Starved and on the verge of hysteria, he suddenly leaped into the ceremonial house through the hole in the roof. Wildly he danced in a weird manner through the house as if affected by some mysterious spirit. Members of the society tried to control the spirit force within him. When he successfully performed the dances and songs of the society, he was elected to membership. To repay the secret society, the boy's uncle gave a potlatch in his honor.

The potlatch was the most remarkable ceremony of Northwest Coast Indians. Tribal life centered around it. The potlatch celebrated not only the initiation of a boy into a secret society, but practically any other event, such as the erection of a totem pole, completion of a house, birth of a son, coming of age of grandchildren, election to chiefdom, or assumption of a new name. Regardless of the original purpose, the potlatch was a strange contest in which the host chief, clan, or village attempted to humiliate and shame all invited guests by ostentatious giving and nonchalant destruction of valuable goods and even human lives. Thus the potlatch was an occasion for a chief to parade before his rival guests his great wealth, prestige, ancestral inheritance, in order to attain a higher social status.

The potlatch ceremony might last several weeks or more. Among the Tlingit, some potlatch rituals in honor of a dead chief took several years to complete. The potlatch could only take place when the host chief had stored up enough wealth to distribute and supplies to feed several hundred guests invited from rival villages. The chief called in all outstanding debts and, because the honor of the village was at stake, the villagers themselves contributed to the potlatch collection. Once the date was set, a messenger was sent to summon guests from rival villages. When they arrived clothed in finest apparel, they were welcomed on the beach with songs and dances and then installed for the period of their stay in village households.

During the feasts, guests were seated according to rank near the host. An official orator, with symbolic staff in hand, thanked the guests for coming and then briefly summarized the event or events to be celebrated. In the days that followed, guests were lavishly entertained. There were recitations and enactments of legends and history by masked and costumed dancers, which vividly dramatized the great inheritance claimed by the chief. There were elaborate feasts served on richly carved dishes, and all invited guests were encouraged to eat well in honor of their host. During the proceedings, specially carved totem poles were erected in front of the chief's house to commemorate the occasion. Speeches explained the meaning of the carvings in careful detail.

Only on the last day were the gifts displayed and distributed. With overwhelming generosity, presents were given to each guest, as speeches stressed their importance and cost. Included in the inventory were large quantities of canoes, clothing, blankets, jewelry, sculpture—all of superb quality. To emphasize his wealth, the chief might also throw precious oil into the fire, burn magnificent canoes or even his own house. He sometimes clubbed his slaves to death with a special killer club and threw their scalps to his guests or used their bodies as rollers for his canoe.

The most expensive gifts were those hammered from sheets of copper about three feet high, one to two feet wide, and no more

than one-eighth inch thick. A T-shape, groove or raised edge usually ran across the front of these "coppers," and sometimes the surfaces were etched or painted with designs of family crests. Coppers might be worth several thousand dollars or equal in value to ten thousand well-made blankets. The chief either gave the copper to his rival as a gift, or else threw it into the fire or broke it into many pieces, just as one might light a cigar today with a hundred-dollar bill.

The potlatch reached its highest expression among the Kwakiutl. In a passionate desire to demonstrate his wealth and shame his rival, a Kwakiutl chief risked becoming a pauper. But this he knew was a temporary condition because his rival had to repay him adequately at a future potlatch. It was unthinkable that a chief or clan should fail in his obligation to repay. To do so would bring disgrace not only to the chief, but to the village as well. When unable to reciprocate for self and public glorification, the chief might commit suicide rather than face ridicule and disgrace. If the chief died, then the obligation fell upon his heirs and relatives.

At its height, when Indians were prospering mightily from the fur trade and had more material possessions than anyone else in North America, the competitive potlatch became a vicious institution. It was an endless cycle of amassing wealth for the purpose of ruining others. In one magnificent gesture, a chief might destroy his entire lifetime accumulation of wealth. His only consolation was that the rival would have to reciprocate with an even greater show of munificence.

When the potlatch was banned by the federal government, the blow struck deep into the structure of Northwest Coast society. Without the potlatch, much of the creative effort given to the costume, regalia, carvings, performance, and even the value given to the gathering of wealth, became meaningless. The potlatch, with its emphasis on family prestige and social position, with its extravagant hospitality and widespread credit system, was at the very core of Indian culture. When it was forbidden, so was the whole way of life that had given it meaning. Native life was halted in one of its primary means of expression. Missionaries increased the doubts and conflicts that Indians felt about their disintegrating world; each person groped to find a new meaning, a new way of expressing life, in the midst of this frustration and resulting chaos.

With rapid white settlement of Oregon and Washington, Indians were removed to reservations. Once disrupted, Northwest Coast culture disintegrated. Commercial fisheries and canneries employed many Indians; others, without income, struggled to survive from small catches of salmon taken from the rivers, much as their ancestors had done centuries earlier.

BUFFALO HUNTERS, TEPEE DWELLERS

The Great Plains, extending from the great river valleys to the high mountains, from the cold Canadian plains to the hot Texan range, played host to many tribes that best typified the popular image of the American Indian. Clothed in fringed buckskin and eagle feathers, mounted on calico ponies, these Indians wildly chased the buffalo and recklessly fought wagon trains, rugged frontiersmen, and army cavalry that crossed their domain. Here were the scenes of the Custer massacre and the heroic exploits of Buffalo Bill, Sitting Bull, Crazy Horse, and many others who figured prominently in the settlement of the Old West. Stories and legends of these Indians, permanently enshrined in our history, have been an unending source of inspiration for books, films, and television programs. Tribes of the Plains reached their full glory in the nineteenth century after other Indian cultures had disappeared or were decaying.

Acquired by the United States in the Louisiana Purchase of 1803, the seemingly boundless, treeless Plains were covered with grasses, shrubs, bushes, and sage; they were exposed to cold snowy winters, hot humid summers, and little rainfall. Open, barren spots were everywhere. From the Black Hills of South Dakota, the highest point in the Plains, as far as the eye could see, the land was flat, monotonous, and surrounded on all sides by the horizon. Across the Plains thundered tremendous herds of buffalo, counted in the millions, and smaller numbers of elk, deer, antelope, wolves, and coyotes. Eagles circled the skies overhead seeking coots, sandpipers, ducks, and small game, while vultures patiently waited to tear what flesh remained on the fallen carcasses of humans or animals.

This vast land had been traversed by many tribes ever since Folsom Man hunted ancient mammoths and bison amid lakes and lush grasslands ten thousand years ago. About five thousand years later, when the climate became drier and the grass sparser, the big animals departed or died. Small groups of people lived in crude shelters or caves and left behind stone points and tools. At the dawn of the Christian Era, the Arikara in North Dakota, the Mandan along the upper Missouri, and further south the Osage and Omaha cultivated corn, beans, squash, and tobacco, gathered wild rice and sunflower seeds, fashioned crude pottery, built earth and log dwellings, and often buried their dead in earthen mounds. The village life established by these sturdy farmers was shattered not by the forces of nature, but by horsemen from the south.

Horses brought to Mexico by the Conquistadors in 1520 were ridden northward for barter or theft, year after year, until after a couple of centuries they were the core of Plains culture. At first, some Indians ate horseflesh. Other tribes trained horses to pull the travois, two long poles whose front ends were attached around the horse's neck while the butt ends dragged along the ground. Family belongings were lashed across these poles, just above the ground. The dog had previously been used to pull the travois, and to many Indians the horse was merely a big dog that transported larger, heavier loads. Thus, tribes often called horses "mystery dogs."

Drawn to the Plains by the horse were the Blackfoot, Sioux, and Cheyenne from Wisconsin and Minnesota; the Crow from the Mississippi Valley; and the Comanche from the Rockies. Of different backgrounds and languages, these tribes restlessly and relentlessly wandered across the vast stretches of the Plains. Sometimes they split into smaller groups or mingled with others to form new tribes. The Great Plains region was indeed a melting pot where diverse peoples joined together in pursuit of the material wealth represented by the buffalo.

The largest beast on the continent, the modern buffalo stood about six feet high at the shoulder and weighed almost two tons. His flesh provided food, his hide was used for clothing and lodging, thus satisfying the numerous needs of a nomadic life. Before the American Revolution about sixty million roamed the Plains like a moving black mass. Because the herd blindly followed its leader, buffalo were easily killed when stampeded by loud noises, waved robes, or prairie fires driving them toward a cliff. When they reached the brink, they had no way to turn back and pressed forward over the cliff. Another method was to drive the herd into a stockade and shoot the animals as they entered. Some hunters disguised themselves in wolfskins, of which buffaloes had no fear, and crawled close enough to shoot their deadly arrows.

Mounted on horseback, the Indian outmatched the speed and agility of the giant buffalo. Stripped to only a breech-cloth and moccasins, the dashing hunter rode alongside the beast and shot his arrows at the heart. Other Indians preferred a lance about nine feet long, which they thrust into the beast. A hunter trailed a long line behind his horse and if unseated, he grabbed hold and was pulled out of danger by his mount.

The buffalo hunt took place between the spring and fall. When the grass was green and migrating herds were expected, families and bands of the tribe came together. Tepees were pitched in a circle, a chief or council took charge, and scouts were sent out to find the herd. When the herd was finally found, after days or weeks, the camp was moved to the hunting grounds. Here the tribe stayed and hunted until the approach of winter and the departure of the buffalo.

When the herd moved on, tribes split into groups and each had to shift for itself. Enough meat for the whole tribe could never be found on the Plains during the winter. Deer, elk, and small game were hunted in the mountainous country or on the Plains, either on foot or on snowshoes. Game was scarce and the people dipped into their supplies of dried buffalo meat stored away the previous summer. All waited the mysterious return of the buffalo, which marked the coming of spring and the rejuvenation of life.

After the kill, the buffalo was carefully butchered and all parts of the body were used in one way or another. The warm, nourishing blood was drunk by the children and the vitamin-packed liver was eaten raw. The stomach was removed and the contents of vegetable matter boiled and devoured. Once the stomach had been

emptied and cleaned it made a fine container for cooking or carrying water. Hunters and their families feasted on the tough, roasted flesh. Chunks of meat were cut from the carcass and sun-dried as "jerkee," or pounded fine and mixed with berries and bear fat to become the staple food, "pemmican." Stuffed into skin bags, this meat could be stored against the lean, hard winter months.

Stripped from the carcass, the fur and skin was cleaned, dried, and smoked and cut into many forms, such as blankets, bedding, clothing, bags, drums, and tepee covers. Skins for the tepee were so well made that they lasted a lifetime. Women owned the tepee and cared for it all year round. Tepee, a Dakota word meaning

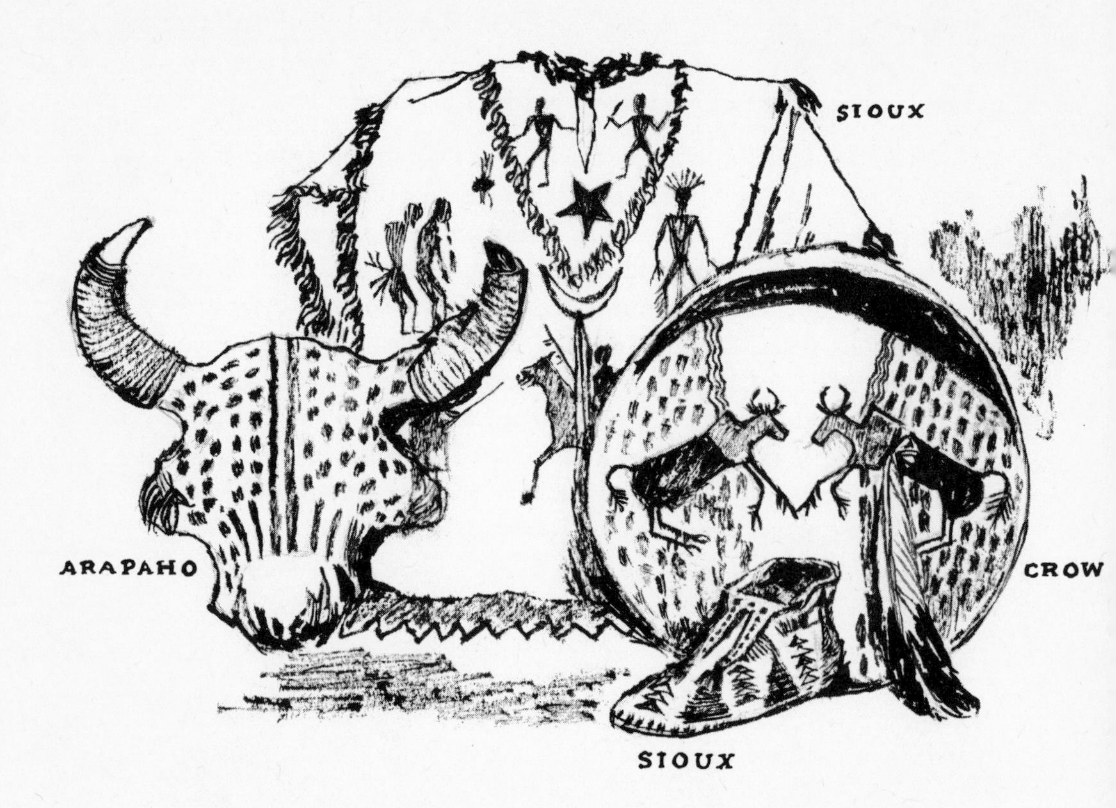

"dwelling," was the trademark of the Plains culture. These cone-shaped structures varied in size and in the number of poles and skins. Most poles were about twenty-five feet long, but the Crows preferred poles almost twice that length. Selected from young pine, cedar, or spruce trees found far from the hunting grounds, these poles lasted many years.

Tepees required about ten skins and were sewn together with wet sinew that made waterproof seams when dried. After the poles had been arranged in a circle, the skins were stretched and tied around with a smoke hole left at the top. With the entrance flap closed, the tepee was warm in winter, and when the bottom cover was raised above the ground, the breezes cooled it in the summer. Women painted decorative designs of buffalo, birds, and geometric motifs on the outside to identify and beautify the tepee. The evening fire made the tepee glow like a rosy lantern, enlivened by the dancing shadows of its moving inhabitants.

Tepees were crammed with sleeping robes, smoking pipes, backrests, axes, bows and arrows, war shields, and countless other items stored in colorful "parfleches." Made of buffalo skin, the ends of the parfleche were folded over to form a strong envelope commonly used as luggage by Plains Indians. Paintings were also made on buffalo robes. Women made geometric designs similar to those on the parfleche, while men portrayed hunts, battles, and visions in lively stylized images of men and animals. There was also the rolled-up skin for the "bull boat," which when fitted around a wooden frame made a waterproof boat for floating women, children, and possessions across streams and rivers. Included in the inventory might be horns fashioned into cups, spoons, dishes and toy tops, skin drums, gourd rattles, bone whistles, shoulder-blade digging tools, and an effective fly swatter made from a buffalo tail.

For festive occasions the Indians wore fringed, decorative buckskin shirts, leggings, and moccasins. Many warriors painted their faces, and some even tattooed their bodies. Feathers attesting to their skill in battle were tied to their hair, adding to their height and dignity. Chiefs were resplendent in breastplates of shell, bear-claw necklaces, earrings, armbands, and a grand buffalo robe. They wore a magnificent headdress of eagle feathers that almost reached their heels and was embellished with mink and ermine fur. These colorful rippling war bonnets best typified the popular image of the Plains Indian.

The men's striking dress symbolized the dominant role that they played in the social life of the Plains. Women worked harder but held a position of little importance. Before marriage, the girl was excused from hard work and preserved her soft hands with delicate quill work. The youth who sought her hand had to present a sizable gift to her brother, usually a number of horses that he had stolen. Some men had two or more wives, perhaps because many braves died in battle and women outnumbered the men. Unlike other, less-mobile Indian cultures, the roaming hunting life encouraged different social systems among the Plains tribes.

The Plains warrior achieved prestige through warfare and enemy raids. Since infancy he listened to tales of valor and the honor of

death in battle. He longed for a chance to fight and raid and boast of his bravery before the assembled village. He fought wars for revenge and more frequently stole horses, but according to a code of rules. In savage bloody battles against white men, he fought for his land, buffalo, and life. In tribal warfare, the Plains Indian placed more importance on touching his enemy than on killing him. He carried a long decorated stick and each touch, or coup (French word for "blow"), was counted; the greatest warriors tallied the most coups. Higher scores were achieved through the dangerous defiance of death than from the accurate shooting of an enemy from afar. Indians stole into enemy villages at dawn and sought to steal the horses kept tethered in front of the tepees of famous warriors. It was the danger rather than the horse that the attacker sought. On the battlefield the highest scores went to those who touched the body of an enemy or somehow managed to scalp him while he lay surrounded by his comrades. Cruelty and torture were uncommon among Plains Indians, and prisoners were rarely taken.

Scalps were taken in great numbers. When dried, they were worn or tied to the top of the tepee for all to see. After the battle or raid, warriors boasted of their deeds in the village while striking a special pole. Each deed of valor was recorded by a coup.

Magic and the supernatural played a vital role in Plains warfare. Indians wore protective charms in battle, but they sought assurance in visions before going on the warpath. A warrior first purified himself in a "sweat lodge" made of poles and buffalo robes. Then he rode out on the Plains, where he stayed for about four days. Here he fasted, thirsted, prayed, cut and gashed his body, and listened intently for signs in the sounds of the wind, leaves, birds, and animals. In loneliness and expectation he awaited the supernatural vision that inspired the confidence he needed.

Power might be gained from ceremonial dances. Most extraordinary of all was the Sun Dance performed by the Cheyenne, Arapaho, Dakota, and other tribes. For this dance, held at the beginning of the summer, a cottonwood tree was ceremonially cut and erected within a large open lodge. Little or no sun worship was associated with this ritual; rather, self-torture was the fundamental feature. Wooden skewers were thrust beneath the chest skin, and the ends were tied to the tree. For hours the warriors danced around the tree, eyes focused upward toward the sun, all the while pulling backwards on the thongs until the pierced bleeding skin was torn from their bodies. The Bureau of Indian Affairs forbade this dance in 1904, but it was revived by some tribes about twenty-five years later in less bloody form.

This action by the Indian Bureau was only the sequel to the final chapter of Plains culture. The death knell had first been sounded in the 1837 smallpox epidemic that swept across the Plains. Then came the gold rush—Black Hills, Pikes Peak—that poured thousands of prospectors onto the Plains, followed by bootleg traders of whiskey and firearms, as well as buffalo killers. The annual kill averaged 250,000, but sometimes these men killed that many buffalo in a single month. Buffalo were slaughtered for the sale of hides, to reduce the Indian's resistance, and, in many cases, for fun. The Kansas Pacific Railroad ran special trains for the buffalo hunt, equipped with food and drink for the "sportsmen" who leisurely shot at buffalo through the open windows. Out of sixty million buffalo that roamed the Plains before the Revolution, only about one thousand survived one century later.

Mutual misunderstandings between Indian and white erupted in bloody battles, climaxed in 1876 with the defeat of General Custer by the Sioux tribe. The army swiftly retaliated. Although the Indians won the grudging respect of some officers as "good shots, good riders, and best fighters the sun ever shone on," the troops split the tribes into small bands and hunted them down to defeat. By 1887, the last warring tribes were gathered into reservations, and the culture of the Great Plains was shattered.

WARRIORS AND POLITICIANS

The Iroquois were the mightiest and most mysterious of the North American Indians. Made up of male warriors and women of fierce and domineering power, they were more important politically than artistically. The name Iroquois originally designated the five tribes in what is now the state of New York—Oneida, Seneca, Cayuga, Mohawk, and Onondaga. When in 1715 the Tuscaroras migrated north from the Carolinas, having been displaced by European settlers, the Iroquois became known as the Six Nations. Other tribes spoke an Iroquois language, such as the Erie, Huron, Susquehanna, and Cherokee, but they were dominated by the cruelty of the belligerent Six Nations. The Iroquois were not only ruthless warriors, but also sophisticated politicians who, about 1570 had formed a powerful confederacy or league.

Ancient inhabitants of New York State, the Iroquois adopted some traits from the Mound Builders to the west and southeast. Surrounding the Iroquois were Algonkian-speaking tribes who also had an ancient history but made little cultural progress. Near the coast the Algonkians usually built dome-shaped wigwams, while further inland, they lived in cone-shaped tepees. They were made up of seminomadic hunting tribes and moved from place to place in small family groups or bands. These tribes rarely came together, had no authoritarian chief, and hence were no match for the dynamic Iroquois tribes.

Like a powerful wedge, the Iroquois battered into the block of Algonkians and split them apart. Whatever strength the Algonkians may have had was shattered and the tribes were forced to move elsewhere. With a firm foothold in New York, the Iroquois increased in number, unified into an empire, and ruled over the northeastern United States.

On the rolling forested hillsides in the Mohawk Valley, the Iroquois built large palisaded villages, which the English called castles because of their resemblance to the medieval walled cities of Europe. Scattered throughout the wooded terrain, these villages were connected by a maze of trails difficult and dangerous for enemies to follow. Many modern wide paved highways still follow the narrow Iroquois trails. Around 1700, about twenty-five villages with a population of between three hundred and six hundred people each flourished in the Mohawk Valley.

Within the log palisade, the Iroquois built huge log-and-bark dwellings called longhouses. Like a modern Pullman railroad car, the longhouse averaged sixty feet in length and eighteen feet in width and housed more than twenty families. Longhouses were constructed of elm bark slabs sandwiched between a double framework of poles lashed together and roofed with slabs of bark laid one atop the other like clapboards. A series of cooking fires stretched down the center aisle, and holes in the roof let in the light and allowed the smoke to escape. Each fire was shared by two or more families who each lived within its own chamber against the wall. Above the shelves and skin-covered platform that served as furniture, hung dried fish, berries, and ears of corn, while utensils, weapons, and clothing hung all over the house. Cured venison and parched corn were buried in watertight bark-lined pits beneath the floor. Although they were smoky and noisy, longhouses were warm and weatherproof.

The Iroquois had few possessions and a limited wardrobe. Moccasins, shirts, leggings, breechcloths, and dresses were made from buckskin and embroidered with porcupine quills and moose hair. Decorative beads were sewn on clothing or strung into necklaces. From the Europeans the Iroquois acquired ribbons, which they often stitched on their clothing, and also silver, which they fashioned into ornaments. Some designs were obviously European inspired, but others, such as double curves and S-shaped spirals, may have been influenced by the art of the Mound Builders.

From beads and clamshells was made wampum, an Algonkian word meaning "white string." Carried as a string or belt, wampum was used as money or as a document. Strings of various lengths covered with an arrangement of dark and light beads were memorized by specialists to help them remember tribal legends and history. As they ran their fingers across the beaded strings, they recited the important tribal records.

Weapons were simple. A brave armed himself with bow and

arrow and a tomahawk with a flat stone blade or heavy wooden ball at one end. A spike or sharp tooth set into the ball end made the tomahawk more deadly. Warriors painted their faces; some let their hair grow long; others wore a scalplock. They shaved off all their hair, except for the ridge scalplock left in the middle and hanging down the back of the neck. The braves were skillful hunters and fishermen and the women were excellent farmers. They raised many varieties of corn, beans, and squash and were among the first Indians to make popcorn over which they poured hot maple syrup. Together with the children, they gathered wild strawberries, greens, herbs, acorns, and other nuts. They tapped the maples for syrup from which they made sugar. Foods were cooked and stored in well-made pottery vessels distinguished by wide broadly scalloped collars often decorated with simple linear patterns.

The clan was the basic social unit of Iroquois society. Clans were all named after totems—animals, turtles, birds, and plants. In this matriarchal society, perhaps inspired by Indian tribes of the Southeast, women owned the fields and longhouse and even supervised the government. The senior woman of the clan, known as clan mother or matron, named the chief or chiefs for her clan. She lived together with her daughters, young sisters, and all their husbands. When a marriage broke up, it was the husband who went home to mother and left the children behind.

The Iroquois believed in and prayed to a productive god, or Great Spirit, who created men, animals, and plants, ruled the world, and was the source of all good things. His adversary was a devil-like spirit called Evil-Minded. According to legend, the Great Spirit and Evil-Minded were originally born as brothers but endowed with different powers. As the Great Spirit was the creator of good, the Evil-Minded created all the monsters, poisonous snakes, and noxious plants. Only if he obeyed and prayed to the Great Spirit could man save himself from the Evil-Minded. The Iroquois peopled the earth and sky with countless other spirits. There was the spirit of winds, sister spirits of corn, beans, and squash; spirit of medicine, fire, water, trees—all under the protection of the Great Spirit. Ritual messages were carried up to the spirit on a column of smoke from burning tobacco and accompanied with much singing, dancing, and music.

In midwinter, when the ground was covered with a heavy blanket of snow and bitter cold winds blew outside the longhouse, the Indians performed the major cycle of festivals. Small heaps of tobacco were burned, people sang, chanted, and danced to the sound of drums and rattles, masked secret societies appeared, and dreams were told. Deeply affected by dreams, the Iroquois believed that dreams betrayed one's secret wishes and feelings of guilt and that their meanings had to be analyzed. During this festival period, a dog specially bred for whiteness of fur that symbolized purity was strangled and burned with tobacco leaves on a wooden altar.

The Iroquois stood in awe before a race of supernatural beings, whom they called Falsefaces. These were spirits or demons without bodies, arms, or legs. They only had faces but with hideous distorted features. Falsefaces could bring disease and death, and to pacify them a secret society was formed. With knowledge gained from these demons, the society learned how to cure many ailments. The members of the society wore masks, carried drums and rattles, and staged dances and rites that frightened away the evil spirits who caused sickness. Their masks had such distorted, fantastic faces that they seemed truly to have come from another world. They had large staring eyes inlaid with shell or metal, arched brows, wrinkled forehead, streaming horse tails for hair, prominent teeth, and a puckered mouth twisted into a smile or grimace and emphasized by a huge protruding tongue. A large broken nose squashed against the cheek like a Picasso picture distinguished many of these masks.

These Falsefaces were carved from living basswood trees. In a plea for forgiveness to the tree spirit for having mutilated the trunk, tobacco was burned and the smoke blown into the branches and roots to preserve the life and help heal the scars of the carving.

Another masked secret society were the Huskfaces, bringers of

joy and abundance. These playful-looking masks were braided from straw-colored corn husks. The eyes were two round holes, the mouth was small, a tiny ear of corn wrapped in husk served as the nose, and the whole face was fringed with corn leaves so that it resembled a sunburst.

The terror reflected on the faces of many masks was also reflected on the faces of many Indians who were enemies of the Iroquois. The Iroquois warriors struck fear into the hearts of their neighbors. They not only destroyed villages, but killed and on occasion ate the flesh of the vanquished in horrible festivals. Prisoners taken captive were driven to Iroquois villages like animals. Anyone who lagged behind was killed. Children and some captives were adopted into the tribe to replace dead or missing Iroquois warriors. Women and old men became servants or slaves. Braves not adopted were subjected to systematic tortures. They were forced to run between two lines of men armed with wooden clubs who beat their bodies unmercifully. Tied to a stake, they were burned with flaming torches, and flesh was gouged out with jagged seashells. The scalp might have been torn off and hot coals poured over the bleeding skull. The victim was rested, given water, and fed during his agonizing torment to keep him alive as long as possible. Indians were schooled to face the possibility of capture. It was a contest, a performance, a drama. Throughout his torment, the victim had to remain impassive, hurl insults at his tormentors, threaten them with tribal retaliation, up to the moment of death. Other tribes learned these tortures, but preferred to use them on the Iroquois.

War was only one side of the Iroquois character; politics was another. About 1570, the intelligent statesmen Deganawida, later assisted by his disciple Hiawatha (he had nothing to do with the fictitious hero of Longfellow's poem), founded the best organized confederacy or league, north of Mexico. Because the confederacy put an end to fighting among the tribes, Indians called it, "The Great Peace." In the following two centuries, the confederacy expanded into an empire that reached from the St. Lawrence to Tennessee, and from the Mississippi through New England. Their power was great over Indian and white. They subdued tribes, pressured states, and allied themselves with the English against the French and later with the Americans against the English. The confederacy was the only Indian nation on the American continent recognized as a sovereign government and never conquered. There are still vestiges of the League of Six Nations among several thousand Iroquois in New York State.

The League consisted of a Council made up of fifty sachems, or chiefs, selected from each of the Iroquois tribes. Sachems, appointed by clan matrons, were given the badge of their lifetime office—an antler headdress. If, however, the sachems were not effective, they could be deposed by the matron, who would hold office until a new sachem was elected. While not permanent officials, women were extremely powerful and influential. Besides the democratic representation of the Council senate, there was another council, much like our House of Representatives, which was called the Pine Trees. Because appointments were based on merit, most Pine Trees were famous warriors, and the group acted as a military council. They influenced the decisions of the great Council, but they had no actual vote.

The League Council met each summer at the Onondaga capital outside of Syracuse. When the League was first formed, the Onondaga Indians were the most powerful and joined the other tribes on the condition that they have four additional sachems, the exclusive right to summon the Council, and the right to ratify all decisions. They presided over the sacred fire kept burning in the Council longhouse and were keepers of the wampum on which the laws of the League were symbolized. The Council longhouse, oriented from north to south, symbolized the unity and geography of the tribes. The territory of the Six Nations roughly conformed to a rectangle. The central fire was tended by the Onondaga, who were centrally situated among the Iroquois nations. The Senecas were keepers of the west door that looked out upon Niagara, and the Mohawks were keepers of the east door that looked out upon the Hudson. Across from the fire at the north sat the Oneidas, and opposite them were the Tuscaroras and Cayugas. An Onondaga Indian was the presiding officer at the meetings.

The power of the League grew as the Iroquois prospered as middlemen in the European fur trade. Councilors were brought to the courts of England and France in attempts to curry favor with the League. When the Iroquois allied themselves with the English and Dutch against the French, they probably turned the course of our early history. Benjamin Franklin had been influenced by the example of the confederacy in his project for uniting the American colonies. Our written constitution, with its federal authority balanced against states' rights, was derived from the unwritten Iroquois confederacy, with its six tribes and democratic council system.

At the time of the Revolution, the confederacy voted to remain neutral. Individual tribes, however, rebelled and supported whichever side they pleased. The majority of Iroquois fought for the British, but a few, notably the Oneidas and some of the Tuscaroras, supported the American colonists. After the Revolution, the Continental Congress agreed to forgive the Iroquois who worked for England. They recognized the League and agreed to protect the Indians and their lands "as long as the grass grows and the water runs." Since that time, state and federal government agencies have ignored these agreements and confiscated Iroquois land. From the original total of eighteen million acres owned by the League, only seventy-eight thousand acres remain today.

North American Indians are not a vanishing race as has been too often assumed; nor are their unique contributions to American culture extinct. It is estimated that the 400,000 Indians living in the United States today will double in number before the end of this century. Oklahoma has the largest Indian population with 110,000; Arizona has 75,000 and New Mexico 50,000. Lesser numbers inhabit the Dakotas, California, Washington, Montana, New York, and other states, where reservations are maintained by the government.

Cultural progress among most Indians has not kept pace with the growth in population. Only those few tribes whose lands were rich in natural resources—oil, uranium, minerals—have made some economic gains. Navaho Indians raise huge flocks of sheep on their ten-million-acre reservation along the Arizona–New Mexico border making them the most affluent tribe. The Cheyenne of Montana, through their own initiative and the utilization of federal, state, and private resources, have made remarkable economic progress in the past five years. Most tribes, however, are depressingly poor by American standards, with little or no income, property, or education. Nevertheless, tribal ties in the form of dance, music, and traditional rituals and arts have held fast.

Although peace was established between the invading whites

and resisting Indians, warfare was replaced by legal battles. Removed from their ancient lands to the confines of government reservations, the Indians too often saw treaties and agreements ignored or revised. The United States Government, yielding to pressures from states and individuals, has broken its word to practically every tribe. Tribal fortunes have been at the mercy of competitive politicians.

Indian reservations and their incomes are held in trust by the United States, subject to federal laws but exempt from state laws, courts, and taxes. An Indian can leave and return to his reservation as he chooses. The problems have been many and the system subject to much criticism. The Allotment Act of 1887 splintered and diminished the original size of more than a hundred reservations. After a block of acreage was allotted to each Indian to farm, the surplus land was put up for sale. This act attempted to convert Indians into farmers, disregarding the fact that among most tribes farming was only women's work. The men hunted, fished, and fought with no knowledge of or inclination for farming. Indians believed that land could be used but never owned. Many tribes lost much land and suffered severely from this ill-advised act, but their loyalty to the United States was remarkably steadfast. Not until 1924, however, and only after they had "proven their loyalty" in World War I, were the Indians granted citizenship in a land they had inhabited for years. This war record was repeated in World War II and the Korean Conflict.

United States policy in Indian affairs was reversed in 1934 with passage of the Reorganization Act, which returned the reservations to the Indians. Under government supervision, Indians of the reservations participated in self-government and were helped to regain some degree of economic and social security. Education, health, the arts and crafts, were encouraged and improved. Some Indians went on from the reservation schools to professional programs and services to assist Indians both on and off the reservations. Church and other missionary organizations have also contributed to the help of the Indian in improving his standard of living and preserving certain aspects of his culture. Progress has been gradual, and much remains to be accomplished for the great society of our original Americans.

Recent studies of the relationship between the Indians of today and their dominating Americans have tried to shape a just and benevolent policy for the future. While perpetuating his many admirable heritages from the past, and maintaining his identity and self-supporting dignity of the present, the Indian strives to make a significant contribution to American civilization. As President John F. Kennedy wrote, "When we neglect the heroic past of the American Indian, we thereby weaken our own heritage."

MOUNDS, TOWNS AND TOTEMS

CHRONOLOGICAL CHART OF NORTH

B.C.	NORTH AMERICA	MIDDLE AND SOUTH AMERICA
50,000–10,000	Man arrives in the New World	Arrival of man
10,000–5000	Archaic food-gathering cultures developed	Emergence of archaic cultures
5000–1000	Copper mined in Great Lakes region; pottery made in the Southeast; corn cultivated in southern regions	Pre-Maya period; Chavin culture, Andes
1000–1	Emergence of Adena culture in Ohio Valley, about 800; emergence of Hopewell culture, Ohio and Mississippi Valleys, about 300; Mogollon and Hohokam cultures of Southwest, 300	Olmec culture, Mexico; Maya calendar and hieroglyphic writing invented, after 353
A.D.		
1–500	Emergence Basket Maker culture Southwest, about 300; Adena and Hopewell cultures at height	Emergence Toltec civilization, Tule; Old Empire, Maya, 317
500–1000	Decline Adena and Hopewell cultures; emergence Temple Mound culture in Southwest; emergence Pueblos in Southwest; Leif Ericson in North America, 1000	New Empire, Maya, 987; Toltec domination of Yucatan; Mochica culture, Andes
1000–1500	Temple Mound culture at height; Classic Pueblo period, 1050; drought, 1276–99, forced abandonment of pueblos; Apache and Navaho arrive in Southwest; Death Cult swept Southeast, 1400; emergence farming villages in Great Plains	Inca Empire at height, 1493; Aztecs establish capital at Tenochtitlán, 1325; Columbus discovery of America, 1492
1500–1800	Decline Temple Mound culture; Spanish exploration Gulf Coast by Ponce de Leon and De Soto 1521–43; Coronado led Conquistadors across Rio Grande, 1540; Iroquois Confederacy established, about 1570; Santa Fe founded, 1610; Pilgrims landed on Plymouth Rock, 1620; American Revolution, 1776; Captain James Cook visited northwest coast, 1778	Cortes invasion of Mexico, 1519; Balboa sights Pacific, 1513; Pizarro captures Cuzco, 1533; Montezuma killed by Spanish, 1521; Portuguese claimed Brazil, 1500: Rio de Janeiro capital of Brazil, 1763
1800–1900	War of 1812; Five Civilized Tribes moved to Oklahoma, Trail of Tears, 1832; northwest coast art at height, 1840–90; War with Mexico, 1846; Civil War, 1861–65; Horse-Buffalo culture of Great Plains at height; General Custer's Last Stand, 1876; most tribes on reservations, 1880	Mexico independent, 1821; Brazil independent, 1822; Uruguay independent, 1828. death of Bolivar, 1830
1900–	Wright Brothers' first plane flight, 1903; Model-T car made by Ford, 1909; World War I, 1917–18; Indians granted citizenship, 1924; Lindberg flew across Atlantic, 1927; World War II, 1941–45; Korean Conflict, 1950–53; Hawaii became 50th State, 1962	

AMERICAN AND WORLD EVENTS

B.C.	EUROPE	NEAR EAST AND ASIA
50,000–10,000	Ice Age caves at Altamira, Spain, and Lascaux, France	Paleolithic Age
10,000–5000	Emergence Neolithic communities	Emergence Neolithic civilizations
5000–1000	Stonehenge, England, about 1500; Aegean civilization, Crete, 3000–1100; Age of Homer, 1100	Pyramids of Egypt, 2780–2100; Aryan invasion of India, about 1800; Shang dynasty, China, 1523–1028; Hammurabi, Babylon, 1800; exodus of Jews from Egypt, 1200; Tutankhamen ruled Egypt, 1350
1000–1	Etruscan civilization, Italy; Olympic Games, Greece, began, 756; Parthenon built in Athens, 447; Alexander the Great, 356–323; Julius Caesar, 60–44	Birth of Confucius, 551; birth of Buddha, India, 563; Assyrian Empire at height, 1000–612; Persian-Greek War, 500; Alexander the Great in India, 329; Great Wall of China, 246–210
A.D.		
1–500	Christian Church founded, 42; Roman Empire at height, 116; Pantheon built in Rome, 118; sack of Rome by Goths, 410; Clovis king of Franks, 481; Constantinople capital of Roman Empire, 330	Han dynasty, China, collapsed, 220; emergence Buddhism in China; Kushan dynasty, India, 50–320; Haniwa culture, Japan, 200
500–1000	Birth of Mohammed; defeat of Arabs at Tours, 732; Charlemagne crowned emperor Holy Roman Empire, 800	Buddhist influence in Japan, 552; T'ang dynasty, China, 618; Heian dynasty, Japan, 784; Moslem invasion of India, about 1000
1000–1500	William the Conqueror invaded England, 1066; Crusades against Moslems, 1096–1270; beginning Gothic Age, 1140; beginning Renaissance, 1400; invention of printing, 1439; Michelangelo painted ceiling Sistine Chapel, 1508–12	Mongol invasion of China about 1280; Ming dynasty, overthrow of Mongols, 1368
1500–1800	Magellan sailed around world, 1519–21; Martin Luther and rise of Protestantism, 1517; Dutch East India Company, 1602; French East India Company, 1664; French Revolution, 1789; publication of Encyclopédie, 1756	Mogul Empire, India, 1526; Ivan the Great, Russia, 1462–1505; Portuguese settle Macao, 1557; Taj Mahal, India, 1632; Romanov dynasty, Russia, 1613–1917; Manchu dynasty, China, 1644–1912
1800–1900	Napoleon Emperor of France, 1804; beginning of Industrial Revolution; Darwin's *Origin of Species,* 1859; *Communist Manifesto* by Marx and Engels, 1848; Franco-Prussian War, 1870	Opium War, China and Britain, 1840; China opened to the West, 1844; Commodore Perry in Japan, 1853
1900–	Nobel Prizes instituted, 1901; World War I, 1914–18; Hitler Chancellor of Germany, 1933; Mussolini in power, Italy, 1922; Spanish Civil War, 1936; World War II, 1939–45; formation of North Atlantic Treaty Organization, 1949; Hungarian Revolution, 1956	Russo-Japanese War, 1904; Boxer Rebellion, China, 1900; Russian Revolution, 1917; USSR established, 1922; Turkish Republic established, 1923; Israel Republic established, 1948; Communist People's Republic of China, 1949; India democratic Republic, 1950

BOOKS FOR FURTHER READING

Collier, John, *Indians of the Americas*. New York, Mentor Books, 1947.

Douglas, F. H., and d'Harnoncourt, R., *Indian Art of the United States*. New York, Museum of Modern Art, 1942.

Drucker, Philip, *Cultures of the North Pacific Coast*. San Francisco, Chandler Publishing Co., 1965.

Griffin, J. B., ed., *Archaeology of the Eastern United States*. Chicago, University of Chicago Press, 1952.

Inverarity, R. B., *Art of the Northwest Coast Indians*. Berkeley, University of California Press, 1950.

Jennings, J. D., and Norbeck, E., eds., *Prehistoric Man in the New World*. Chicago, University of Chicago Press, 1964.

Josephy, A. M., ed., *The American Heritage Book of Indians*. American Heritage Publishing Co., 1961.

LaFarge, O., *A Pictorial History of the American Indian*. New York, Crown Publishers, Inc., 1956.

Lowie, R. H., *Indians of the Plains*. New York, McGraw-Hill Book Co., 1954.

Martin, P. S., *Digging Into History*. Chicago, Chicago Natural History Museum, Popular Series in Anthropology, No. 38, 1959.

Martin, P. S., Quimby, G. I., and Collier, D., *Indians Before Columbus*. Chicago, University of Chicago Press, 1947.

Morgan, L. H., *League of the Ho-De-No Sau-Nu or Iroquois*. New Haven, Human Relations Area Files, Vol. 1, 1954.

Myron, R., *Shadow of the Hawk*. New York, G. P. Putnam's Sons, 1965.

Ritchie, W. A., *The Archaeology of New York State*. Garden City, The Natural History Press, 1965.

Roe, F. G., *The Indian and the Horse*. Norman, University of Oklahoma Press, 1955.

Silverberg, R., *The Old Ones*. New York Graphic Society, 1965.

Spencer, R. F., Jennings, J. D., et al., *The Native Americans*. New York, Harper and Row, 1965.

Swanton, J. R., *The Indians of the Southeastern United States*. Washington, Bureau of American Ethnology, Bulletin No. 137, 1946.

Underhill, R. M., *Red Man's America*. Chicago, University of Chicago Press, 1953.

Willey, G. R., *Prehistoric Settlement Patterns in the New World*. New York, Viking Fund Publications in Anthropology, No. 23, 1956.

Worthington, H. M., *Prehistoric Indians of the Southwest*. Denver, Denver Museum of Natural History, 1961.

INDEX

ABOUT THE AUTHOR

ROBERT MYRON is a professor of fine arts at Hofstra University on Long Island. His interest in the North American Indian began at Ohio State University, where he worked on his doctorate degree in the field of the ancient mound-building Indians. This book is an expansion of his interest in the archaeological past and the cultural present of Indian tribes. Dr. Myron is also the author of books on prehistoric art, pre-Columbian art, and the Italian Renaissance. He is also editor of a series of books on the history of art. Dr. Myron lives with his wife and two sons in Hempstead, New York.

1 2 3 4 5 70 69 68 67 66

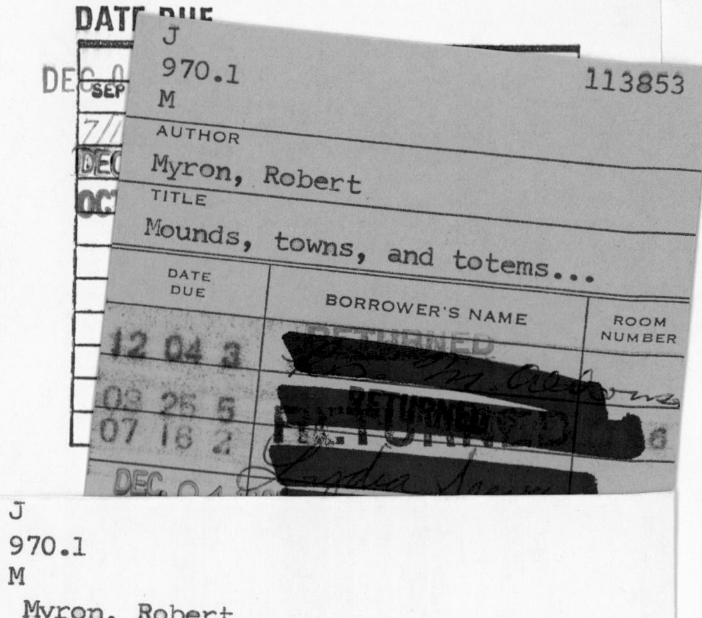
DATE DUE
J
970.1
M
113853
AUTHOR
Myron, Robert
TITLE
Mounds, towns, and totems...
DATE DUE
BORROWER'S NAME
ROOM NUMBER
RETURNED
RETURNED